Activating Compassion

Letting Go of Judgment and Creating Love, Joy, and Peace In Everyday Life

Activating Compassion

Letting Go of Judgment and Creating Love, Joy, and Peace In Everyday
Life

Jesse Ann Nichols George

Table of Contents

Acknowledgements

Thanks to the many individuals that have been a part of my path. Some have passed and some are still with me. I appreciate those willing to mentor me along the way. I have much gratitude for the friends that have come, gone, remained in my life and gave me many experiences on my journey. To my family who never gave up on me, believed in me and helped me when times got tough. To Ralph for providing encouragement to follow my passion, embrace it, and bring it to life. You have all held a special part of my life and I appreciate you being there while I have taken this journey.

Preface

When I think of how compassion has played a role in my life, what I find is that it has woven in and out. Sometimes I was receiving it, sometimes I was giving it. It shifted forms, appeared at unexpected times, and seemed unavailable at times I thought I needed it most.

Growing up I knew compassion through the love of my parents. They seemed to have an endless amount of it; and no matter how much I thought they had no idea what I was going through, in reflection now I can see that even if they didn't understand the specific situation they did know the feelings and frustrations that were present. What a lesson this is to realize that we don't always have to know the specifics to be caring and understanding with others. What a gift to realize that we can still offer our heart and love, our support and be a friend.

As I got older and found my interest turned to boys, falling in love, doing my own thing compassion wove in and out differently. Mostly I was too selfish and wasn't very compassionate. Like most teenagers and young adults it was all about me and what I was getting or not getting from others. I did offer compassion and help friends through things they were going through; yet at the same time I could be completely ruthless, judgmental, and very harsh with others.

In reflection I simply didn't take the time to be a little more patient or considerate of what was happening with others. I would like to write it off as being young and reckless. If I understood that someone was dealing with a problem I could be very understanding and kind; but like many young people it is easy to judge people and get angry and upset because someone was driving too slow, or took too much of my time, or kept me from doing something I wanted, or placed restrictions on me in one way or another. Sometimes I wonder when I reflect back how those around me dealt with me. It is amazing that I had any friends at all at times.

While I embraced my spiritual journey early in life I had so very much to learn. Even though the concepts were in my head, I can't say the lessons really sunk in until much later. The danger in this space is that I thought I was being compassionate when in reality I was still living under so many judgments and frustrations that things were not working out in my life. I thought I was protected because I was on this spiritual journey; but in reflection I see that I knew only a small fraction of what I thought I knew.

In this space I was trying to be more compassionate; but could never see where I wasn't being that way. I was so set that I was doing the right things, yet couldn't see the damage I was doing to others. I remember at one point I had a retail store with bulk herbs, essential oils, crystals, books, etc. I was doing healing work, teaching classes, and manufacturing my own products. Unable to truly see how I was blocking my own process, and not being responsible in my actions my business was not able to survive and I had to file bankruptcy.

I felt that the world had given up on me. I felt betrayed by the universe. Trying to make the business work ended up bringing ruin to 2 relationships and my health. Make that 4 relationships if I count two that got away because I couldn't look past my immediate issues.

My health was taking a huge turn for the worse. I remember it taking me 2 hours to get out of bed in the morning because I couldn't feel my legs and couldn't stand on them, and I couldn't see past the end of my bed. I was scared to drive because I didn't know when my vision might go out completely and unexpectedly. This was one of the big wake up calls in my life. I was in my early 30's and decided to make a move leaving the beauty of the Central Coast of California for the desert of Arizona.

I knew that I could give up and face being in a wheelchair for the rest of my life or take the chance to try and heal myself. To me I had to try to heal. I took time off to simplify my life and to focus on myself and my own journey for awhile. I missed the healing energy of the ocean but knew I needed to take this journey of living in the desert.

Off and on during my time in Arizona I worked to get my life back in order. I went in and out of trying to develop working in the spiritual arena, meeting with minimal successes. In reflection I realize that my focus was more on what I could get than what I was giving. Although at the time I couldn't quite see it. I kept helping people and doing healing work, created my own line of energetic candles, and even started offering quantum energy work to help people manifest their desires.

While I know my heart was in the right place I just hadn't broken completely into how to fully give and be compassionate of others. I admit I was getting better; but I was still so far away. It seemed like I kept getting one growth experience after another; and I could really feel my heart opening more and more and more. So while I would not consciously choose to return to Arizona, I was blessed with many wonderful connections that blessed my path and helped me refine and develop myself. It was in the last couple of years in Arizona that compassion started to break open in my life. One of the first turning points was when my dad had his first stroke. It really opened me to how limited our time is here on earth. This man had showed compassion to others all his life. His passing is one of the greatest impacts of my life. I wasn't able to truly say good bye to him; his health took a sudden turn for the worse and I was not able to make it to him before he passed.

I had just come off of moving into a new place and had my identity stolen only a month prior and then lost my father. The pain was overwhelming. Every emotion must have ran through my body, mind, and soul. It was in this stage I could feel myself open further than I had ever known. I could feel my heart opening so wide. It was only a few months later I chose to move closer to family so that I could have any time possible with my mom in her later years.

It was in this space that I found myself fully vulnerable, fully open, and ready to face the fears of fully putting myself out there to help others. While I may never fully perfect compassion; I know that I am truly living from a space of compassion. I have come to realize that I want to provide my gifts and wisdom and tools to others. I want others to have the life that they dream of, the life that inspires them to create and provide their gifts to others.

I know that we can find fulfillment, bliss, and all that we want through compassion. It is from this foundation that I offer you this book so that you too can discover for yourself the satisfaction from activating and living in compassion. Through this book I offer you the opportunity to create the life you want building rewarding relationships with others and yourself.

The Hidden Enemy

I recently was asked how a person can create their reality when the news and others bombard us 24/7 with negative information. Even with the law of attraction and saying mantras or other things, there is still a sense of being bombarded with fears. This is interesting to me because if I was to look at the people saying these things, I would never know the intensity of what they are experiencing. It is as if they have accepted that this is how their life has to be. There is a sense of feeling powerless and overwhelmed.

What is sad to me, is the number of people that feel this way. However, I can't say that I have always been immune to this thought pattern. I too have had times in my life where I couldn't see the light anywhere. I remember lying in bed literally paralyzed by the fear and worries I had, wondering if I could ever get my head above water. It felt like I couldn't get oxygen into my lungs, I was scared to make changes, scared if I didn't make changes, afraid to trust anything or anyone, my mind was rampant with worries and wondering how I could possibly ever overcome the pressures.

I tried to turn my mind to something positive and to pray and meditate and everything I could think of; but it felt like nothing would fall into place for me. I was frustrated and feeling inadequate; all I could think of was that I was a failure, that I must have done something horrible to try to help others, only to be in great devastation myself. It felt like God and the whole universe had shunned me and turned away from me. What I hadn't accepted was that in this space I was the one that had disconnected from Spirit, the very thing that could help me.

Although I was so certain that I was trying everything that I could, in reality I was being passive. Spirit and the Universe was patiently waiting for me to step up and join in the wonderful existence that I was dreaming of and wanting and longing for. I couldn't see how much I was sabotaging my own efforts and successes.

Like many people in this state all I really wanted was a little compassion from Spirit and the Universe. It seemed like all the efforts I put in brought me nothing; and I couldn't afford to spend tons of money getting to where I wanted to be. Every option seemed out of my reach or unavailable to me. It was sheer anguish having a passion and desire to make a difference in the world and feeling there was no way to bring it to reality.

The piece I was missing was that I needed to give compassion instead of demanding it. For it is when we give compassion in those states of desperation and exhaustion that we receive compassion. What I couldn't see is that there is a very huge hidden enemy that blocks us from having this compassion. This enemy is multi-faceted and can be a few clouds on a sunny day, a blinding blizzard, a tornado ripping through our life. This enemy manifests in our doubts, fears, worries, pain; sometimes coming from within ourselves and sometimes without. It is so tricky that it even makes us think that it is our own thoughts or destiny.

This enemy tries to infiltrate into every fiber of our being. It comes into us through every experience that we have. It comes to us from family, loved ones, friends, co-workers, and everyone that we come across. Sometimes it moves from us to others, and other times it moves from others to us. It can create triggers within us that get activated years after the trigger occurs.

I realize you may be feeling a little like you can't ever get away from it when it is creeping in everywhere, often times undetected. You may be wondering if you can ever break free from it and leave the grips that it has on you and your life. I reassure you that you can have your freedom, and you can clear it from your life no matter how rooted it is. You can move forward without it.

By now you are probably wondering, so what is this monster lurking around you? It is simply called judgment. While sometimes judgments are very obvious; many times judgments come in very subtle forms which manifest as blocks, fears, worries, anxieties, pain and so on. As a matter of fact most judgments that we have we don't even think of as a judgment.

So in order to understand this hidden enemy let's start by taking a look at what it means. Dictionary.com offers the following definition of judgment:

"the forming of an opinion, estimate, notion, or conclusion, as from circumstances presented to the mind"

The word judgment can take on many connotations. For the purpose of our work here the above definition provides a good foundation to work from. A judgment forms through experiences and circumstances that occur in our life. It can come from something experienced through our senses, emotions, and base of understanding. Judgments can form from a single moment or experience or from a pattern or set of experiences.

The tricky thing is we may not even realize we have formed judgments about things until we hit a block or challenge. While many judgments are formed from knowledge or experience; others are formed based on an assumption. For example we see someone that is very overweight, often times a judgment is formed that the heavy person is not physically active and sits around eating junk food all day. Judgments formed from knowledge or experience often times will have a larger impact on us personally. This may be evident with someone that wants to be rich, but was raised to believe that rich people were snobby, controlling, and mean. This conflict comes from the formation of a judgment that we will become those things if we get money, and that judgment creates a block that keeps us from earning money.

The good news is that judgments are not facts or truths, they are an opinion or perception that we have accepted as truth at some point. What we have done is to make an association between two things and shut off all other possibilities and options. In the example above money got associated with negative attributes; because they have been connected money becomes a negative thing that we resist. So even if we consciously want it, we resist it because we don't want the attributes that we have associated with it. When we get to where we can remove the negative attributes and separate the item from those negative attributes we remove our judgment about it.

Once judgment has been removed from negative attributes we are open to receive all possibilities. We can change our experiences and develop a relationship. With our judgment gone we are now able to enjoy money and the things it can do and bring into our lives. We automatically open ourselves to unlimited possibilities, since we are no longer restricted by the judgment that money will turn us into a bad person. With a loving relationship to money we are free to improve our circumstances, follow our passion, share our gifts with others, help others, we are free to create a new reality that we enjoy.

One focus to keep in mind when clearing judgments is that nothing in and of itself is good or bad, nor will it make us good or bad. The choice of how we are going to be and act is always ours. I have known people with no money at all that constantly hurt people. Just look at the news, many crimes are committed by people with nothing. This of course can lead into a whole other discussion. On the other hand there are many people that have lots of money that give and give and give to help others. Money or the lack of money does not make us be one way or another. We choose how we will be and how we will treat or interact with others whether or not we have money.

So you may be wondering, if judgments are so abundant in our lives how do we ever get free of them? How can you defend yourself from this hidden enemy? Kind of like a nasty parasite judgments can appear to be gone and then show up when you least expect it. Fortunately, we can rid ourselves of judgments and move ourselves into a life filled with happiness and peace. The remedy is strictly up to us and is completely free.

Before we look at the remedy let's get a little better understanding of the judgments we make and how they may be formed. Judgments that create blocks in our life come from where we made a decision that we cannot have something, aren't good enough for someone or to do something, that we are limited in what we can have. It is a narrow point of view that keeps us from having a positive relationship with others, ourselves, and everything in our life. In essence judgments stop us from creating. When we are blocked from creating we often become bored or unfulfilled and start a cycle of trying to find happiness without ever really finding it.

Judgments might include some of the following thoughts or statements:

People like me never get that

I will never be able to accomplish that

I can't live the life I want

Love never works out for me

Money is always scarce in my life

Nothing ever works out for me

People don't like me

No one wants me to be on their team

My coworker is horrible and mean

My brother doesn't care about anything other than his inheritance

Fat people shouldn't go out in public

Old people shouldn't drive

When we look at these statements some of them probably sound very harsh to you; yet every day, people are saying and thinking these very things. They feel like a helpless victim to their circumstances and the people around them. They feel hopeless because they have created a judgment that doesn't allow for another possibility.

The statements above are not only hurtful to many people; but are not the truth, or have more to the situation than what the initial statement is based on. The key to getting out of judgment is to have compassion. Compassion is like the magic potion. Compassion opens the door to all possibilities, there are no limits, anything can be created from a space of compassion. All major religions refer to compassion as the way and the one thing that removes us from "sin".

It is important to keep in mind that compassion is about understanding and accepting where a person is at. It does not mean that you agree with them or see things the same way. It means that you are willing to entertain that things can be different than they are through understanding the pain or fear that is underlying the judgment.

Let's take a look at the statements above and see what happens when we apply compassion to the situation. How much will it change how we feel about ourselves or others? How will it change the outcome of the situation?

Starting with people like me never get that. You can fill in what that is for you. This statement shows the person to have decided that they cannot have something that they really desire. This person has a judgment that no matter what they do they cannot have what others have. If this person was given compassion we would understand that there is pain from feeling the desired outcome is out of reach. When we start to ask questions of compassion, we want to know what kind of people do you mean? Just because others have not had it, why can't you? There are many successful people that have come from the ghetto, or lived in shelters; but it didn't stop them.

In compassion we acknowledge the pain and see that there is also a fear of achieving the desired result. This fear may come from an attachment that this person will become something or someone that they don't want to be if they make the achievement. However, when we realize that we can have the achievement in a way that works for us, we let go of the judgment around it and can decide if we actually want the desire or not.

Looking at the statement I will never be able to accomplish that. Again we see a fear of succeeding. We should ask why not? In reality it is possible if we are willing to be persistent and build the tools we need to accomplish it. For example someone says I will never be able to accomplish getting my PHD. Why not? Because I need to work and support my family and I don't have the time to do it or the money to do it. What if you could do it for little cost and would only take 1 or 2 days a week at 3 hours a week? Well that would be possible. The fear behind the judgment is cost and time; however, when the fear is reduced or eliminated the judgment disappears and is replaced with self confidence and a sense of realizing accomplishment is possible.

Jumping to the statement people don't like me. Here is a judgment that there is something wrong with me. There is a fear of not being accepted and a desire to protect oneself from further pain of being teased or outcast. In judgment the outcome is loneliness from not wanting to trust others. With compassion we see that this person is awkward when relating to others, and has not had people in their past understanding and accepting that awkwardness. Realizing that we all do things or say things that don't come out right from time to time, and that if we offer a space of safety where someone can be themselves and then support them as they open up; this person can go from awkward to being a great manager or speaker or anything else. They can have as many friends as they want.

Let's look at the thought fat people shouldn't go out in public. The judgment is that fat people should not have the same rights as other people. It comes from a space of fear and being uncomfortable with someone that has a lot of weight, and sometimes a fear of becoming fat ourselves. There are judgments that the fat person has total control over their weight and that they want to be fat and just aren't doing anything about it. In compassion and getting to know that person, would it change your perception if you knew that person ate a balanced diet of healthy foods and worked out every day; but due to an allergy, glandular problem or other health issue may not be able to reduce their weight no matter what they try?

The point is there is so much more beyond our judgments, and that judgments are easily cleared when we look at what is holding them in place and seek to really understand what is happening. Imagine if everyone accepted you for who you are? What if you removed the judgments you have for yourself and others? How would your life be different? What if everything that stands in the way of what you want didn't exist?

Take some time to think about the judgments that you have of yourself and others. Then apply compassion to the situation by really understanding it, looking at the fear or pain that is at the base of it. Ask the questions needed to understand it and then ask what would life be like if that judgment, fear, and pain didn't exist? Ask about the possibility of things being different, what if you could do what you wanted? Ask what do you need to do to make your desire a reality?

When you ask these questions the universe will respond. The cool thing is you don't even have to know how it will happen you just have to accept that it can happen and then ask to be shown what to do to make it happen. How great is that? What are you going to make happen that you have blocked from doing? How will you look at others differently without judgment? What if everyone applied compassion?

Not My Problem

How many of you have ever said something like "it's not my problem that person is fat", "it's not my problem he/she is afraid to make a commitment", "it's not my problem you are unhappy", "it's not my problem you hate your job". I would say if we are being truly honest with ourselves, almost everyone could say that they have at least thought if not said one of the above statements or something very similar to someone. It may have happened when you were younger or it may have even been quite recently.

Regardless whether the statement is true or not what we really want to consider here is the response to the situation. Of course people do need to take care of their own issues. They need to make their own breakthroughs and accomplishments. However, how we respond to the issues that person is dealing with and how we treat the individual is our opportunity to make a difference.

When we make judgments about that person and blame them for doing what they did and make them feel bad for their choices and actions; we have actually stepped away from Spirit and are now being selfish because we are only thinking about how it affects us without any consideration for what the other person is going through. When we take a compassionate approach we realize that their choice or action may not have been the best; however, we also realize that they may have meant to do something else or may have had many things going on that created stresses or other things that led up to them making a poor decision. In compassion we recognize that there is more than what we can see.

The key becomes that we realize that even if we can't do things for them, that we can offer kindness and support and remind them that they can make things different if they want.   The person that is really living in a compassionate space will go further to offer assistance to help them get there. For example you cannot work out for the person that is overweight; but you could agree to walk with them or go to the gym with them. Even if you don't have the time to do this – you can encourage them with positive reinforcement when they do go.

Let's look at an example of someone that gets pulled over for speeding. It is easy to think "serves that person right they shouldn't have been speeding". Is it your problem to deal with? No. Can you keep them from speeding in the future? No. Can you agree that it sucks to be pulled over for speeding? Yes. If you were the one pulled over instead of that person, how would you feel?

When we address this from a space of being with or without compassion we get the following situations. Without compassion we enter selfishness and judgment; this may even lead us to feel as if "justice has been served" because they got caught. While being pulled over and ticketed may be what that person needed to make a change to not speeding; it does not mean that we have to celebrate or rejoice in that person's mistakes. With compassion we can simply say something like "wow, that is a drag", "hopefully, that person will be ok and whatever led them to take that action will be cleared so that they don't have to go through that again."

The reality of it is we don't know all the details that led that person to speed. What if they were speeding because their spouse or child had just been taken to the hospital? This is not about justifying the actions of others; but it is about understanding and accepting that there may be so much more to the situation than what we see or know about.

Learning to be compassionate is about stepping outside of our judgments and selfishness to stop and pause for a minute and ask ourselves how we can make a moment or situation better? Again this is not about doing the work for someone else, it is about how can we change something from a negative experience to a positive experience. One thing to keep in mind in this process is that we don't have to agree with the choices of others; but we can still be caring of what they are going through.

One of the challenges I see with people learning to be compassionate is when that person finds something easy to do, it may still be difficult to be caring with those that are challenged by things. Here I ask that you learn to realize and accept that we all have different strengths and challenges. What is easy for us may be very difficult and scary for someone else and vice versa. Wouldn't you want someone to be patient and understanding of your challenges?

For example, you may find it very easy to multi-task or call and get information from a company or ask for something to be corrected on an account you have. However, for your spouse he/she procrastinates on doing these things until the last possible minute; because they are not good at speaking with people under pressure. You may find it challenging to do a lot of socializing or making a bunch of small talk with others; while your spouse thrives on these communications as they feel they can learn about the world through others.

We all have things that are easy for us and things that challenge us. Keeping this in mind when we see others having a challenging day, or dealing with unpleasant things takes us one more step towards living a compassionate life. Think about how you would feel if someone did something to help you when you are in challenging times. When we lend a helping hand to those that are experiencing challenges we also strengthen our relationship with them and raise our own personal vibration.

Let's say you weren't feeling well and a neighbor offered to go to the store and pick something up to make you feel better; wouldn't you feel closer to that neighbor? On the other hand if you had a neighbor that said "it's not my problem you are sick, you should have things around your house for when that happens"; would you feel a greater separation from that neighbor? What if you came home from a challenging day at work; would you rather your spouse say "that's not my problem you had a bad day, get in the kitchen and fix me dinner" or would you prefer your spouse say "I am sorry to hear that happened to you today would you like me to take you out to dinner so you don't have to cook, or go get something and bring it home, or I could cook tonight so that you could relax?" My guess is you would prefer the latter; at least I know I would rather have the understanding spouse over the demanding one.

One of the big lessons, when we choose to activate compassion in our life, is learning to create and build relationships with others instead of separation from others. Now does this mean that you have to give up doing everything that you want to do in order to do something for someone else? Not at all; but I will be addressing that more in the next chapter. Does it mean that you have to be best friends with everyone around you and become available 24/7 for the rest of the world? No. Now that may be your choice and that is fine; but it is not an obligation or pre-requisite for activating compassion in your life.

Realistically, there will always be people that we connect with more than others. We are never going to please or change 100% of the people 100% of the time. As a matter of fact, we are not here to change others; however, we can give them an example of another way to be. We can be a vehicle for change. When we look at being a vehicle for change, we allow our decisions and actions to have an impact on others; giving them an opportunity to choose something different or enhance what they already have.

For example, opening the door for someone that has their arms full sends a reminder to others that there are people that care. It can trigger a sense in the person that the door is opened for, that someone does care about them. This one simple action could change someone from a grumpy mood to a happier mood. It can also reinforce that doing good things for others also brings good things to you. This could be the case for someone that has been helping others all day and then receives help from someone else. Appreciating the action reinforces how good they feel when helping others and to want to continue to do that even more.

What is exciting is how many lives can be affected by one simple little action. Let's look at how this happens. A woman is late getting out of work to go meet her husband for dinner with important clients of his. You choose to hold the elevator for her. As a result she is able to relax and make the dinner on time. As a result of being on time her husband is able to relax and provide a better presentation to the clients. As a result of his confidence and warmth in presenting things the client agrees to do business with him.

The husband is happy and provides the waitress with an extra good tip. This tip helped the waitress make her rent that month. As a result of having the rent on time the landlords were able to make upgrades and repairs. The client having secured a strong business deal is now able to hire additional employees for this business deal. As a result of hiring more employees one employee is able to keep his house from going into foreclosure which saves his marriage and keeps his family from having to impose on others for help. As a result of his marriage doing better his wife is less tense and receives a promotion and drops 20lbs of weight keeping her from having severe health issues.

The key here is that a simple gesture that took only a few seconds out of life ended up affecting many lives in a positive way beyond what we could see in the moment. What if you got to know that a one minute kind gesture saved someone's life or kept someone from being evicted from their home? Would you do more one minute kind gestures? One of the beautiful things about compassionate action is that it keeps on giving and giving and giving. It affects us and the person we are giving to and so many others.

This pattern is sometimes known as a cascading effect or the butterfly effect. The interesting concept here is that what we give to others keeps giving and expanding. When we look at the interrelationship we share with others what we give to others is also what we want others to give to us. This doesn't mean that we want that exact thing; however, it does show that when we give kindness to others we want others to be kind to us.

This is an interesting concept to think about that whatever we do or give to others is what we are asking for. This works on negative things we do to others as well. When we get angry and mean towards others, we are asking for others to treat us this way. The universe does not differentiate between good and bad but it does register the vibration. So if we choose to be on the vibration of hate then the universe sees us as wanting hate. If we choose to be on a vibration of love or joy then the universe sees us as wanting love or joy.

When I think of how one simple action can have a much larger impact than the immediate moment, it reminds me of some of the lyrics of a hymn song titled "Pass It On".

"It only takes a spark to get a fire going,

And soon all those around can warm up in it's glowing;

That's how it is with God's Love,

Once you've experienced it,

You spread the love to everyone,

You want to pass it on."

The line "It only takes a spark to get a fire going" reminds us that we are a spark and we can create the fire that makes things happen. It starts with us and we can become a warming glow that provides warmth and brings people together, or we can become a raging and destructive fire.

The phrase "that's how it is with God's Love" reminds us that God, Spirit, Universe (whatever term you like to use) does not judge us and is always doing small and large things to help us have a better day. "Once you've experienced it, you spread the love to everyone" is a reminder that when we feel good and are happy and loving we share that with everyone around us. Everyone that we are around will get to experience those good feelings.

Finally, the line "you want to pass it on" goes beyond just wanting to share it with others. This reminds us that when someone does something good for us that it is important to pass on doing something good for someone else. The best thing we can do is to appreciate the gift of kindness, and when the opportunity presents itself, be kind to someone else.

I remember seeing a movie once where a woman had become homeless and the owner of a company bought her lunch and gave her a job. Not because he was taking pity on her; but because he wanted to do a kind deed. Later in the movie the woman does the same thing for someone else, and explains that someone had helped her at one time. At the end of the movie the guy that originally helped the first woman had actually been helped by her before she became homeless.

Sometimes we cannot return a favor to the person that originally helped us; but there are many opportunities to help others in our own way. The story above brings to light a great point that we never know when a person we help might be able to help us at some point. For me I think that it is like anything in life – seize the opportunity to do what you can today, because the opportunity may not be here tomorrow.

When we take advantage of the opportunity to help someone the benefits will overflow in other areas of our life. This happens because the universe sees that we want to use the opportunities we are given to create something positive. When we do this the universe wants to give us more opportunities to create and have enjoyable experiences. It is this principle that explains why people that are "lucky" keep having fortunate things happen; and why people that seem to have things going wrong keep having things go wrong.

What if you could change things from rough to easy, bad to good, sad to happy by taking advantage of an opportunity to do something good for someone? What if brightening someone's day with a smile or thank-you made everything flow smoothly in your day? This happens all the time. So the next time you feel like nothing is going your way, open your eyes and see if there is something you can do for someone. It doesn't have to be much, it can be as simple as a smile or saying thank-you, or appreciating the people in your life. A sincere act of kindness without expecting anything in return can change your world to something truly amazing.

So the next time you think "it's not my problem that _____", stop and think for a moment if there is anything you can do to do something kind for that person or to help them in some way. It is a strong way to start activating compassion in your life.

What About Me?

It seems that no matter how evolved one gets on their path; at some point during the process comes the question "what about me?" Many times I have seen people start on their path excited and charged only to hit a period where they go through feeling drained, empty or lost within themselves. Now the thing that makes this question even more difficult is that there is often times guilt that goes with having this question come up. It is the guilt of feeling that when we are on this path this question should never have to be asked at all.

I am here to say stop beating yourself up. I absolve you from all your guilt. What is going on when this question arises is that you are in need of setting boundaries for yourself. No matter how evolved someone is they still have a need to receive. Even gurus or monks need time in prayer or meditation or to simply sit in quiet and receive.

The difference is that the caring you receive changes. People may not always express their appreciation or think to stop and ask if they can give something back to you. When you are at a stage where you are doing lots of giving to others, you are much like a parent who gives to young children. Those children are excited and happy for what you have done; but they don't stop and say what can I do for you mom? This doesn't happen until after those children grow up.

So the caring is actually coming through, even if it is not the way that we anticipated. There may still be many of you saying this is all fine but I still want someone to do for me some of the things that I do for others. I assure you that this is something that comes in time. Your actions are actually providing an example of how others can be too.

Let's go back to those children. They grow up seeing your example day in and day out; and even if they don't implement cleaning their room up on their own at the age of 7, eventually they do get to a point where they do it on their own because of the example that you set for them. Just like with children sometimes you have to tell them what you need and want from them. If you don't tell them then they just don't know or don't think of it on their own.

So many times these days we expect others to do things without ever letting them know what we want or expect or need from them. It is like we just expect people to read our minds and do things. On occasion we drop subtle clues, not realizing that this can be even more puzzling. What if your boss expected you to do a project but never told you that you needed to do that project. Then suddenly gets upset at you because you didn't do it; and when you say you didn't know you were supposed to do that get a reply saying you should have known you had to do it because it was related to the area you handle.

This is where I look at the old adage "ask, and you shall receive". How can you get what you never asked for? This breakdown of communication is probably most evident in our personal dating or marriage relationships. If I had a nickel for every time I heard "he should have known to do that" or "he should have known I needed that". First of all no matter how close your relationship, communication is key. Putting pressure on someone to read your mind is a judgment that is going to create more separation than union in your relationship.

If you really truly want or need something, ask for it. The clearer you are about your needs and wants the easier and sooner you can get those things. It is not about what you should or shouldn't have to do to get something; it is about whether you actually want it. Others and the universe want to give you what you want; the sooner you ask for it the sooner you can get it. There is no shame in the asking; and most people will appreciate knowing directly. Playing twenty questions to get information out of someone tends to be draining, frustrating, irritating and pushes people away.

Now with that being said let's go back to looking at our personal dating or marriage relationships. Ladies let's face it most of the time men genuinely are not picking up on things you want and need; they need you to blatantly tell them what you need or want, leave behind the "he should be able to figure it out" mentality. Your hidden resentment that he isn't figuring it out, is going to end up pushing him away. Men don't wait for the woman in your life to have sudden mood shifts before you start communicating with her. Checking in with her periodically to just see if there is anything that she needs or wants could save you from stepping on a land mine in your relationship.

Just as I mentioned in the chapter before, how you act is what the universe is going to give to you. So if you are doing lots of giving the universe will keep working on bringing people into your life that will give to you as well. You will also become naturally magnetic and draw in people that want to give. You will also draw in more people that will appreciate what you are giving them. Remember the pass it on effect? The people you receive from may be different than the ones you gave to.

Another aspect to consider is the one of having boundaries. While it is important to give, you need to also set boundaries to respect your physical, mental, emotional and spiritual boundaries. If you are giving to the point that it is costing you your health, state of mind, and the essence of who you are it will get harder and harder to give and you will have less and less to give. This means that you need to balance your giving with the things you need to do to take care of you.

This brings me to the next point. If you want others to give to you, then you must first give to yourself. When you do things to make yourself feel special and that feed and nurture you on every level, you will raise your own sense of self-worth. When you raise your self-worth, others will also find you "worthy" of giving to. Remember that "giving starts at home". This means that you are "home" and you must first give to yourself.

When you give to yourself you will find you have more to give others and can do it easier. When you feel that you are taken care of, you can give more freely and truly of yourself. For those of you that are concerned about feeling guilty for giving to yourself; please think again. What if you were actually being selfish by not giving to yourself? When we learn to give to ourselves and make certain that we are taken care of; we can give even better to others.

When people learn how to be secure enough to give to themselves on every level, they also develop a strength and confidence that enhances what they give to others. This is like getting a good night's rest and eating a good breakfast so that you can be alert and functional at work. If you only got 2 hours of sleep and didn't eat any breakfast; your body would be struggling to stay awake and your mind would miss things and you are likely to be grumpy with others. However, if you got 8 hours of sleep and a great breakfast you are ready to face anything the day brings to you.

Now if you were to add into that getting a good workout in or snuggling up with the one you love and perhaps giving yourself extra time to start your day without being rushed; you are likely to be in an even better mood that makes you more willing to help others and more relaxed about what you face during your day. If you take this further and make certain you are taking time out to have fun on your days off and take a vacation from time to time or do other things you enjoy, you begin to get to a point where nothing is a big deal and you are offering more of yourself to others.

I am certain that you can see how taking care of yourself puts you in a space where you are able to be more of your own potential while accomplishing more in less time and providing more to others without resenting it or feeling like you are sacrificing everything of your own. The key here is don't wait around for others to give, they will get on the bandwagon soon enough. Your cheerful attitude will also be a catalyst for others wanting to give more to you.

Now there is a final concept that I would like to address here. People that are givers actually have a hard time receiving, even when they want to. They are so used to giving that they turn down others that do things for them without even realizing it. Perhaps you or someone you know who is a giver receives an offer from a friend to pay for dinner or to run some errands for you or to help you with something. The reactionary response that I hear so many times is "oh, you don't need to do that", "it's ok I can get it", "I don't want you to do that let me pay you back or contribute", "no, please don't do that".

All of these statements show refusal of a gift. Imagine if you gave someone you knew a present and they told you "no thanks, I don't want this." How would that make you feel? How often would you keep trying to give them a present when they did this? When you say the above statements you are doing the same thing. Keep in mind that one of the best gifts you can give to someone is to let them give.

People feel good and it raises their energy vibration to give. See it is important to let others give because it helps them rise to a more rewarding and enjoyable life. What better gift can you give to someone? When they raise their vibration they give more to others, and so on. The more people that give, the less individuals feel burdened or weighed down with the "responsibility" of doing so much for others. It is like evening out the workload so that everyone is sharing in getting things done instead of just one or two people doing it all.

Think about the areas that you can start letting others give to you. Take time to communicate clearly with those around you so they understand what you need and want from them; remember they want to give you what you want, they really want you to be happy. Ask yourself how you can give more to yourself, and thus make yourself a person that others want to give more to.

Remember you are worthy and deserving of receiving and it is as important as the giving.

No More Pain

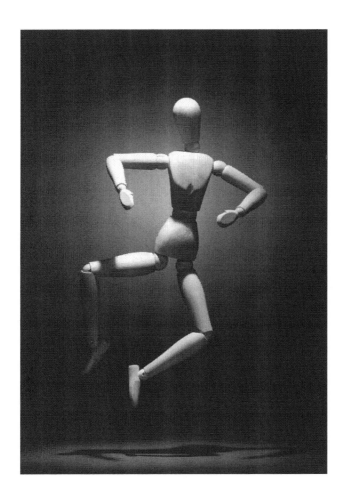

One of the questions that I have gotten from people that have actively started on their path or have yet to start on their path is "why do I have to go through so much pain?" "Why do I have to hurt so bad, when I am doing so much to help others?" "It seems like the more I help others the harder my life is". Perhaps you have had these thoughts or similar ones. I know that I have wondered some of these very things.

Each one of us is born with innate gifts and talents to share with this world. Each one of us has a message that drives us, motivates us, inspires us and at times even angers us. It seems like almost everyone that is sharing their gift with the world has been through hard times, difficult experiences and painful challenges. These experiences, however, have led them to have even more to share with the world. It is these very experiences where some of their most powerful understandings have come from.

Those that have gifts of intuition, premonitions and are empathic have some of the most intense experiences as they have to learn how to sort through what are their emotions and what emotions that they feel belong to others. History has shown that saints went through a great amount of suffering just so others could have a better life. The question remains do we have to suffer to make a difference in the lives of others? Does the process have to be painful? How much must I endure?

The answer isn't as clear cut as I would like it to be. As mentioned before many seem to have many experiences that are very intense. The key is that the "pain" tends to be a phase. It is only a segment that helps us move fully onto our "path" and sharing our message with the world. Often times the stronger the "pain" the stronger and more important the message you have to share with the world.

When we start to view things this way, we can come to realize that the pain is there to motivate us to do and be more in this world. It is there to help us to choose a path that offers us everything we could ever imagine and even more. The key here is choice. Spirit wants the path to be our choice. Spirit wants us to live an amazing, full, joyous, and peaceful life.

Just to clarify, Spirit does not cause us the pain associated with getting there. The pain is what results from not embracing and using our gifts for the betterment of all. It is an accumulation of energy. It is energy that is gathering in one spot with nowhere to go.

This is like a pot with boiling water and a very tight lid. If the lid does not have a place for that boiling energy to go, the pressure can blow the lid off or cause the water to boil over creating a mess, eventually it can cause the water to dry up and then cause the pan to burn or catch fire and be consumed.

Using our gifts is like using the hot water to cook food or make tea or sterilize something to make it safe to use. Resisting or not using them can cause destruction, frustration, drain from cleaning up messes, and yes pain. Now some may think "I don't want these gifts," "I can't handle this anymore," "how can I get rid of these gifts?" Again I think most that have broken through this phase can say that they either thought of giving up their gifts or felt like they were too much to handle.

As I mentioned earlier those with the gifts of intuition, premonition or being empathic are often times hit particularly hard in this process. The reason for this is because they do not get to choose what they see or feel. Often times what they see is something that they cannot stop or do anything about. Many times they may even go through getting physically ill, experience emotions out of nowhere, and see what feels like horrors. Imagine knowing that a tsunami would hit and destroy a country. You can't stop the tsunami, you can't change the devastation or the lives that will be ruined or lost; but you feel all of the pain and emotions of everyone going through it.

This is what people with these gifts go through all the time. Not always on this magnitude, but it happens quite regularly in their life; often times on a daily or at least weekly basis. These people often times have the hardest time finding the right outlets for their gifts.

My message is don't give up on your gift. The key to stopping the "pain," that goes with your gift, is not giving it up; but is in finding positive outlets for the gifts. First, you want to learn how to tell what you are seeing and feeling applies to you and what applies to someone else. This takes lots of practice and learning to ask questions such as "who does this belong to?"

The next step is to start asking, how can I share my gift with the world? If you ask this question every day you will begin to get answers and pieces of information to help you. The universe responds to provide you answers to help you figure it out. This often times comes in subtle (or sometimes not so subtle) ways. For example, you may find an article or meet someone that has dealt with what you are dealing with. Sometimes you suddenly get an idea of something to do, or get inspired. You may have a friend forward you information on people that are using the same gift you have.

Once you look at what is coming your way, you will get the next piece and the next and the next. It is like the universe is leaving you a trail of clues to get you to move towards utilizing your gift. The beauty of this is that while it is giving you information to help direct you or give you clarity, you still get to choose how you will bring it out into the world. You get to decide the channel that most interests you.

There are many options for using your gifts. Some may choose to do psychic work. Others may choose to help solve crime cases. Other choices could include helping others to be prepared for disasters, doing workshops, writing books, and so much more. There are so many different avenues for helping others.

As you begin to use your gifts to help others, the pain will go away, and you will find that you get feelings of joy and happiness and fulfillment. All of this simply because you chose to share your gift. The key is finding a way to help others with your gift. Doing so brings to mind the old adage of "help others and you help yourself."

Another part to getting past a stage of "pain" with your gift is to implement balance in your life. When your gifts are developing it is important to make certain you have a good diet, get plenty of rest, take time for yourself. You will find it valuable to have time alone as well as with others. Time alone and time in nature will help your mind clear and give you "breaks" that you will need to help you feel refreshed and ready to work with your gifts.

Many that I know, myself included, have found as their gifts are developing that it gets harder and harder to be in large crowds of people. For the empathic person it can feel like there are hundreds of people talking to you all at the same time. Eventually, you will get to a point that you are ready to deal with the crowds as you start sharing your gifts with others.

The difference is that when you are doing a workshop, the people around you are there to make improvements in their life or within themselves. You also get to decide the environment and length of time that you will be in that environment. Knowing that you are choosing the situation and letting the intensity out through speaking and giving a focused energy; allows you to manage and actually get to a point where you can enjoy it.

Even once you develop your gifts to a point where you can manage and enjoy them by sharing with others, it is still important to take even a few moments a day for you. It is important for you to take vacations and enjoy the beauty of this earth. Doing so will help you renew, refresh, and continue to get inspired over and over again. This is the lesson of balancing doing with receiving. If you forget to take time to receive, the doing can grow stagnant and the pressure can build up again.

The pauses give us a chance to be in gratitude. Taking time to get our own experiences give us more to share with others. It gives us the chance to be in enjoyment and pleasure. We need moments of peace and serenity; for they are the food that nourishes us and gives us strength to continue to move out of the pain and into sharing with others.

Now some of you may be feeling really inspired about now; however, others may be feeling a bit overwhelmed with this. There may be several questions running through your mind such as what if I don't want to do workshops? Speaking in front of crowds scare me. What if I don't know how to write a book? I don't know anything about putting myself out there. How am I supposed to do this when I don't have money to spend on this and I am just barely getting by?

There may be many more questions besides these. First of all let's step back a little. You don't have to be there today or tomorrow. You don't have to know how to do everything. There are going to be some fears that will need to be faced along the way.

To begin with the only thing that you have to do is choose to use and share your gift to help others. No one expects you to become a guru overnight. Keep in mind that the universe only gives you what it knows that you can handle. You get to decide where you are going to start with it.

Take another deep breath; because you also don't have to know how to get there. The universe is going to take care of the how for you. Yes, you do still have to put in the effort and do the work; but the universe will take care of most of the details for you, as long as it knows that you are on board. All you have to do is use the situations that the universe gives you.

Let's look at facing the fears that come with feelings like you don't know how to do things. There are many ways to develop your skills, just start researching it. Some of you, may be afraid of speaking in front of others. Most people are; and actually most of the biggest gurus were afraid to speak in front of people. You might not know that by looking at them now; but they were when they were getting started. Many of them still get butterflies before a workshop or speaking engagement, even after doing hundreds of presentations.

The only difference is that they have chosen to face their fears. This is done by placing your desire to help others and share your gift as more important than the fear. Once you begin to face the fears you have in moving forward, eventually you will get to a place where you get excited by what scares you; because you realize that you have something amazing to give to others. Use the love you have to help others to get you through.

Eventually you start looking for what challenges you, because there is a rush in getting past a fear. It is exhilarating and a great sense of accomplishment to know that you have moved past what has held you back. As you get more comfortable with this process it will get easier and less scary. Like anything the more you do it, the more secure you are with doing it.

Finally, something that goes hand in hand with facing our fears is being afraid of failing. This is very real and very genuine. So the only real way that you can truly fail is to give up and never try again. However there are things that we can keep in mind regarding this.

For one, you are not going to appeal to 100% of the people 100% of the time. The point is to learn who are the people that are interested in what you have to share. Even more than this, focus on your gift and see who shows up to receive it. It is not about shoving something down someone's throat. There is no one way for everyone. Some people will follow you forever, some will use some of what you have to share, some will be with you for a short time, and some will want to know how they can do what you do.

Another thing to keep in mind is that you are human and you will make mistakes. Those mistakes are not there to destroy you; but are there to help you learn where you need to refine things. Our mistakes help us to become even better. They are like the grains of sands that create a pearl. They can be annoying, frustrating, irritating; but they polish us, show us what we were missing, keep us on track.

Keeping these things in mind can remove a lot of pressure from you while you are developing your gifts. Learning to work with your gifts is much like learning how to drive a car. It can be overwhelming when you are getting started, you may have a couple of accidents and feel it is too expensive (aka painful) to drive and want to give it up. However, when you persist and refine those driving skills you find that there are incredible places you can get to and things you can do. Your desire to see more than what is in your own backyard and to reach out to others becomes greater than your fear of getting into an accident. Eventually you learn how to avoid accidents, you get better at driving, and it becomes enjoyable.

Finally, take things one little step at a time. Some days you are going to feel like tackling big chunks and some days you need a break. Often times you will find it easiest to break things in to smaller manageable pieces. Start by asking yourself what can I do today?

This will help to bring you into the present time. You might have 50 things on your list to do; but you may not be in a position to implement them all right now. So ask what can you implement within the next week. Out of those choices ask yourself which would you like to start with.

This is not just about looking at what is physically possible; but is also about looking at what you feel you can handle on an intellectual and emotional level. Many things can be done without spending any money. With today's technology we have so many more options for starting things and how to put our gift out there.

If you get stuck, find someone that has succeeded in what you are doing. Use that person as a resource. Most of the time those that have already made achievements will be more than happy to help you make your accomplishments as well. They know what it is like to be in your shoes, and they want you to have your own successes. They want you to find as much enjoyment in life as they have.

Your journey doesn't have to be painful. The pain is like the storm before the rainbow shows up. It is a call for you to share your gift. The universe and many others support you in stepping away from the pain and into a life that you can truly enjoy. Your gift is wanted, desired, and needed.

From the principals of my Genesis Clearing Statement, you are safe, you are supported, you are loved, you are able to be joyous, you are able to be peaceful, you are Divine Will.

Gimme Gimme Gimme

Now you may be wondering what this has to do with compassion? You may be thinking isn't it selfish to wonder what you are going to get instead of what you are going to give? At first glance it is easy to perceive it that way, but not everyone that asks what they will get from doing something is being selfish?

As an example let's take a look at someone that comes up to you and says will you give me $10,000? While some will simply say "sure, here you go" and never ask a question most people are going to ask why or wonder what it is needed for. It is natural to ask what you are going to get for something. Would you go to work for a company without asking what that company can offer you? You naturally want to know what you will get for giving your time to that company. If you like it you continue with that company, if you don't you find another company to go to work for.

Asking what you are going to get for investing your time in becoming compassionate is a natural question and it does not make you selfish for wondering. When we look at this process there are both tangible and non-tangible things that will appear in your life. I am not going to lie to you, there are times that there are no immediate results for your actions. As a matter of fact, many times what you get will not come through the person you are being compassionate with at the moment you are being compassionate.

The exciting thing is that you are likely to be able to receive so much more than what that person can give you. For example, let's say you had a friend who's car broke down and needed a ride to work and you agree to take them. That friend may not have anything but $2 to give you. Let's say that you are not interested in their $2 and it doesn't begin to cover what you spent on gas getting them there. On the way home you were thinking how you could really use some help taking some things you no longer want to the thrift store; but don't know how to transport everything because you have some things that are too big to put in your car. When you get home a neighbor asks you about some items that you have stacked up (the very ones you were planning to take to the thrift store) and offers to drive you there and load and unload everything.

As you can see the universe provides you with something that you really need as opposed to you having to take something that you don't need. So when we start to look at what we will get for our efforts this is only a small example. Receiving is the natural counterpart to giving. When we give we let the universe know that we enjoy the experience of giving. We experience the higher level of vibrations, which put us closer to spirit, by giving; and we want others to know this great feeling. Our desire for others to know what it is like brings people into our lives that can give to us.

There is an old lore that says that you will receive 3x-10x what you give out. This could be 3-10 things or it could be 3x-10x better than what you gave out. So by doing a favor for someone can bring 3-10 others that do a favor for you or a favor that is 3x-10x greater than what you gave. Again you may not always get it in the way or time that you plan; but it will always come at a time that you need it or that could be very useful for you.

So sometimes this is a non-tangible thing like someone paying you compliments or lending a helping hand; and sometimes it is tangible such as getting a promotion or unexpected money showing up in your life. Let's look at a more tangible example of how this principle works. Let's say that you give someone $10 to get some food. Over the course of the next week 7 people give you $10. How much would it change your desire to give if you knew you could make 300% - 1000% for every dollar you spent?

What if you helped one of the neighborhood kids fix their bike; and within the next week someone sends you money to get the car repairs done that you have been putting off for the last 3 months? This is what happens when you are compassionate. Think about how you are with others. How much more are you willing to help someone that is always helping someone else as opposed to someone that is stealing from you? Most likely you are going to want to help the person that is always helping first.

Now before too many uproars get going here, let me say that one is not worthier of being helped than another. Sometimes the person that is stealing needs help more than others; however, what we are looking at is simply where you desire to give. It is human nature to want to help those that are giving so much to others. There is a saying "you can never give too much". It is true in that as long as we are in a giving space we are also always receiving; and since we receive more than we are giving we really cannot give too much.

Now I already hear people saying "but I give and give and give; and I am still struggling, why is that?" There are a couple of things that play into this. Sometimes we are not receiving because we are giving not to give but only to get something. This is about expecting to receive and this comes from a space of manipulation instead of compassion. You can tell the difference here by asking yourself would you do this if you were not getting anything for it? If you can truly answer yes to yourself then you are giving from a space of compassion.

Another part of giving and not seeing anything is asking yourself what are you truly giving to? This leads us to need to ask additional questions as in do you truly support what you are giving to, or are you giving to something that genuinely helps someone improve themselves. So let's say you give someone $100; however, you realize that person is going to use the money to buy drugs instead of food or pay their rent. Here we try to rationalize that we are helping this person; when in reality we are not helping that person. In addition aspects of ourselves mentally, emotionally, and spiritually are in conflict with giving to something that is destructive to someone.

When we become in conflict with our actions we create blocks within ourselves. This conflict and supporting of destructive behavior pulls us further away from Spirit. Remember when we are pulled away from Spirit, we have made a choice to separate from what feeds, nourishes, and provides us with our dreams and desires. So a guideline that you can use when trying to decide if you are in conflict with your giving or not is to ask yourself "can I support this?" "will this lead to creating something good or will it lead to something destructive?" If you can support it and it is creating something good you are with Spirit.

This aspect can overlap the concept and principles of "tough love" that became so big in the 1980's. The key here is finding a balance. These days many kids have gotten in trouble with the law, tried drugs, or made other choices that were not to their benefit. Everyone I know has made an unwise choice at some point in their life.

So the key is that the people on a destructive path are often times crying out for help, and have things that they need to work through. The fact is that someone may have made one bad choice that has had long residual effects in their life. I do not believe in totally turning our backs on people; however, we do not need to support their destructiveness. There are many that have done jail time and turned their life around. There are many addicts that have kicked their addiction. The difference is that they also chose to help themselves.

The key is we want to be a source that helps people to be able to thrive on their own and take care of themselves instead of giving in ways that enable people to continue to be dependent upon others. With this concept what we are looking at is that it is better to help someone find a job that allows them to get their own car, then to always be transporting them everywhere. It is fine to help them out a time or two; but if they make no effort to improve their circumstances then it is time to stop being their chauffer and to start teaching them how to create the resources to have their own car.

This can be very hard to do especially when it is with someone that you care about. Anyone can hit a period of hard times and need some assistance; however, the question becomes is that person continuing to try to make changes or are they sitting around not doing anything to change their circumstances. When this is a spouse it is a little easier to gauge if this is a pattern or not. The key is learning how to be tough while still offering support. This may involve making certain an unemployed spouse is actually trying to find work and not tolerating them sitting around doing nothing. At the same time provide encouragement that they can see things through and that they can find something that will work out.

As we look at this it is a fine line between helping and being taken advantage of when helping others. It is important that when helping others you also keep your own boundaries. This may even mean being "selfish" at times. Let's say you have a friend that is having hard times so you give them a place to live while getting their feet back on the ground. You come home from work one day to find them dealing drugs. This is an example of needing to be selfish or needing to set boundaries and let that person know that you will not accept such activity in your home.

While you may want to help this person you cannot put yourself or anyone else in your house in jeopardy because of their choices. You could lose your home and everything else in this type of situation. You have to become "selfish" in an incident like this because if you do not have a place to live or look out for those that live with you such as a spouse or children, you will not be able to help others. In this example not only is the person being helped unappreciative of what they are receiving but they are being very disrespectful.

So when we look at this, when operating from compassion you have the opportunity to receive everything that you could want, desire, and even more. The more you give to something that you can support the more Spirit will be in your life and the more you will receive. When you give to those that are creating positive things instead of those that are being destructive, you will receive many times over what you have given. So when you want to know what you will get; you will get more than you can give.

Blind, Deaf, and Defensive

So many people feel that the road of compassion is all blissful, joyous, and full of blessings. In the bigger picture it truly is. However, sometimes what is truly a blessing isn't always comfortable when we are receiving it. I can't begin to count how many "awakened" people have really been in a "dead sleep".

What I mean by this is that many people start on their path to "enlightenment" with a joy, they feel that they have learned so much, and at times are even arrogant. They have gotten so good at looking at the areas of improvement in others, but do not look at or deal with their own areas of improvement. There is a sense of accomplishment, which leads us into a false sense of feeling that we know so much more than others.

I see that particularly in this time where so many people are becoming an expert in something. Many feel that they have the "cure" or the "tool" or the "answer" to whatever you need. It is easy to get lost in the glory of creating something great, and at times to become complacent in our successes and achievements. What is not easy is to admit that no matter how much improvement that we make that there are always areas that we can still improve or work on.

These areas are often times very sensitive. They are like a bruise that you can't see. These are areas of our life where we feel the most vulnerable or the most inadequate. As you grow and develop yourself on any path it is easy to want to discard the comments of others or to take insult to their observations, perceptions, thoughts, and viewpoints of you.

When someone hits one of our sensitive areas it is easy to first deny it. This denial is being blind to something that exists in our sphere. Now it is true that the other person may not be seeing everything, they may not know your history, they may just be critical because of their own inadequacies that are being triggered around you. However, you would not deny their insights unless that sensitive area is needing care and attention.

The key is not how much truth there is in something as to learning why the other person has that perception. It is about being open enough to learn from their observations and see what in you is creating it to be viewed differently. For example, you put on a blue shirt and someone comes up to you and says "why are you wearing a purple shirt?" You know that you are wearing a blue shirt; but others are not seeing it that way. It doesn't matter if the shirt is actually blue, when 20 other people view it as purple that is how they are experiencing what you are wearing. The key is to learn that it appears as purple to others and to know the effect that is having on them.

Now you may choose to be around people that can see the shirt as blue, or you may choose to learn that what appears blue in your house when you put it on may look different when you get outside around others. If you can learn what makes it appear purple, then you can learn to use that to your benefit and make any necessary adjustments to either help others see the real color is blue or to learn how to work with it being a different color in other places. So open your eyes to see things not only as you know them, but as others see them.

When working with others it is important to keep in mind that what you are seeing is not necessarily what someone else knows or intends to present. Find ways to open their eyes gently so that they can see things through the eyes of others. It is a reminder that we may not always know the truth of something based on a moment's perception. Let's say you see someone else's shirt as purple and they insist it is blue. They invite you over for dinner and when you arrive at their house you see that their shirt is clearly blue. When walking the compassionate path, you are willing to see what others are seeing; but also are willing to see the truth and what others know to be true.

In addition to being "blind" and resistant to what others see we have another challenge. This is the challenge of being "deaf" or not listening or hearing what others have to say. It is hard to hear what appears to be judgments from others, or to listen to someone about meditation that has never meditated before when we have been doing it for 30 years. The reality is that everyone has a valuable piece of information to give us if we are willing to listen to it.

The person who has never done meditation has information just as valuable to provide as someone that has done it for decades. Let's say you are providing a meditation class and for several years the techniques you use get lots of positive responses; and then one day you are doing a new class and someone that has never meditated comes to you and says that something you say or do during the meditation is very disturbing to them. Now while we are not going to please 100% of the people 100% of the time this can be a great learning experience for both of you.

If you are willing to listen, you can learn that perhaps you need to rephrase something. It can also be an opportunity for you to provide additional teaching for this new person so that they can better understand why you use a particular method. Let's face it, these types of situations are great for helping us to freshen things up and to realize just because something has worked in the past doesn't mean that it is still working today. This part of being compassionate is realizing that sometimes we need to listen to others so that we can grow. What if the thing this new person is questioning has actually bothered several people, but they just never said anything about it?

So when you get someone that is telling you something that you don't want to hear, take a moment to thank that person because they are giving you a chance to become even better. They are giving you the opportunity to create additional options to help more people. This doesn't mean that every suggestion is reasonable for you to implement; but every suggestion is worth listening to and seeing if there is something in it that could be useful to you.

When working with others there are times that we really have to tell them something that they don't want to hear. Let's say your boss is rubbing people the wrong way, and it is creating a group of people to want to sabotage your boss. You realize that your boss's intention is not to come off this way, and that your boss feels that they are simply doing what needs to be done to take care of things. It is very unlikely that your boss is going to want to hear that they are causing problems among the employees instead of creating a productive work environment.

You get up the nerve to tell your boss. When coming from a space of compassion, it is important to acknowledge and recognize that his intention is to help and not harm. It is about coming from a space of caring about what is happening and that your boss may lose their job over something completely unintentional. Letting your boss know that you realize he is trying to improve things, but that many employees are finding his actions abrasive and are even trying to sabotage that boss; gives that person the opportunity to make a change or to clear things up.

It is possible that person may not want to listen or hear what you say and may not make changes; and then they have to deal with their choice. It may be that they don't seem to accept what you are saying and then give it thought and make some changes. It may also be that this person realizes the value of what you are saying and finds a way to not only accomplish what needs to be done; but to do it in a way that others can support them instead of resist them.

If your words fall on deaf ears, then you have at least provided an opportunity for a different outcome. On the other hand you may end up opening a door of gratitude by allowing a change to occur. If someone appears not to be listening to what you have to say, be willing to step back and give things some time. Your input may appear to fall on deaf ears; but it may be that person just needs some time to process the information that you gave them. When they first got the information from you, it may have created a state of shock and that shock needs time to wear off before things can be looked at. The key here is being patient and to provide the person you are sharing information with some processing time. You may find that person, once they have had time to process the information you gave them, will come back to you and ask to get your help and insight and feedback in order to gain a better understanding of things. So just because you don't get an immediate response don't give up on things.

The next part of giving and getting information that we are not ready for is the aspect of being defensive. This occurs when the information is presented in a way that seems attacking. This often times can shift from hurtful to valuable, by simply shifting our perspective or presentation of the information being given.

Let's say someone comes to you and says you are mean. It is easy to react and say "no I'm not mean." This may get inside your head and repeat itself over and over again. Without even realizing it you have become completely defensive. This happens because there are feelings of being attacked. What if we changed from our defensiveness to inquisitiveness? What if instead of arguing with the person presenting the information to us, we ask "why do you say that?" or what makes you feel that way?"

This simple shift in our perspective takes the other person off of the offensive, and places them in a position to express what is truly bothering them. It may not be that they really think that you are mean at all. You may find that person has felt powerless most of their life, or may have been in an emotionally or mentally abusive relationship. These past experiences lead them to become rebellious and to push back in the areas of life where they feel like they have a chance of having control over their circumstances.

You may also learn that a particular action that you are doing is coming off different than you intended. Finding out why you are perceived that way can help you improve on how you present yourself to others. Imagine how quickly the "attacking" person would change if you stopped and thanked them for bringing that to your attention, and engaged their opinion of how to change that and let them know that you didn't intend to come across that way and are glad that you know so that you can make a change. Your appreciation and willingness to understand their perceptions will bring value between you that allows you to have a rewarding connection with that person.

Now what about when you find someone else becoming defensive about what you have to say to them? When someone is getting defensive then it is important to realize that what you are saying sounds attacking. It is true that they may be in denial about something; but more likely it is because they are feeling attacked. This can often times be avoided by simply gathering your thoughts briefly before speaking to them and rephrasing what you want to say in a way that is more comfortable for them to accept what you are sharing.

If you say "you are a horrible boss and you are going to lose your job if you don't change" is not very useful and will make your boss probably want to fire you. If you say "I notice that you seem more tense than normal, and during the meeting people were getting very nervous because they thought you were upset with them when I know you weren't. I know that you want the best working atmosphere possible for the employees here. Let me know if you need to talk about anything, or if you would like my assistance to make things smoother. I know that you can do it, but if you would like any assistance so that you can focus on other things that you need to take care of, I would be happy to help you." Can you see the difference here?

You see just shifting things a little in how you approach someone makes all the difference in showing them that you care about them not only as a boss but as a person. You show that you are not just another complainer or critique, but someone that is interested in making things better for everyone. This simple little shift could be the difference in everyone dreading coming to work or everyone looking forward to seeing their co-workers, and having a work environment that is enjoyable and supportive.

Now of course you want to learn to understand the person that you are dealing with and what will work or not work. This can be a learning process of it's own. However, the lessons that are learned in the long run and the relationships that are built from being compassionate with what others may be experiencing, feeling, or thinking can become rewarding for everyone involved. When you develop this space of safety and openness for everyone involved true growth can occur and amazing things will be created. Imagine how much more can be done and how much further we could go if we all cared a little more about others.

So the next time others are communicating with you and you with others, stop pause and see what you can do to create something positive out of the situation. Remember to take your blinders off, your earplugs out, and don't take things so personally. Be patient with others while they learn to open their eyes, become willing to hear things, and find ways to present things in a less threatening manner. I know you can do it and you are likely to find that once you do it a few times that it isn't so hard to ask a couple of questions or offer some help. Like many things it gets easier the more that you do it.

Waking Up

When people are ready to start on the path of compassion it is much like when someone starts a new gym membership or exercise program or anything else. There is a tendency to get a little bit of a sort of adrenaline rush by how good it feels. It is new and exciting and people tend to go further into it than they are able to accommodate.

Like other things that we do, there is a tendency to pull back completely. My suggestion is that when you start on this path start small with things that can be completed in short periods of time. Try giving a neighbor a hand for a couple of hours, working in a soup kitchen once a week, volunteering to coach a soccer team or anything else that interests you. The key is to start small and then stay with that for 2-3 months before taking on something else.

There is always room to build. There are a limitless number of people and groups that need assistance from volunteers. Sometimes I like not being committed to any one thing and simply seeing what each day brings me. For those of you that have full schedules already this can be a great way for you to get started.

In this format you are simply available moment by moment for what comes along. There are many opportunities in any given day to be compassionate with others that take little or no time out of your day. I like responding in the moment to a need. It becomes a spontaneous act of kindness that is often times very meaningful to someone else.

First, let me say it is important to not be harsh on yourself for missed opportunities. These are the opportunities that you don't catch in the moment and later realize that you should have done something. Like anything it takes practice to build your awareness. This is much like waking up in the morning. You don't go from a sound sleep to being fully awake and moving. It takes time for your body and mind to wake up, and it is also this way with learning to be compassionate. Remember it is important to be compassionate with yourself as well as others, especially when you are getting used to being in that space.

It is also important to keep in mind that while you may be excited to help someone or be compassionate, that they may not be ready for your help or to receive your compassion. It is important to respect this space for them. In this situation it is best to give them an open door policy to come to you at a later time.

This is much like any relationship where two people start dating. We will call them John and Jane. John needs to take things at a slow pace because his last couple of relationships didn't go well. Jane wants to show John that she is a great girlfriend and is compassionate to John's past of being left by girlfriends that were never available to him.

Jane contacts John several times a day; but instead of making John feel more comfortable he feels like it is too much. John asks Jane to not contact him as much. If Jane continues to contact John in her attempt to be "compassionate" she will drive John away. If Jane can let him know that she understands and will respect his request and lets him know that she will let him contact her (and reinforces this with action), and as he feels comfortable doing it then John is going to feel like he can trust and open up to Jane. They then go on to develop a great relationship because John has an open door to discuss things with Jane as he needs and without pressure.

The key here is that we want to focus on making the offer, but not forcing others to take us up on that offer. We want to be in a place where we are ok if they accept it or don't. Remember it is not personal if someone does not take you up on your offers of kindness. Some people really need to work through things on their own.

An example of that is when you have 2 different people trying to sell you something. One sales person is very pushy insisting that you take a particular item even though you don't want it. Knowing you can't get out of the store if you don't take it, you finally give in. Later you either return the item or stuff it in a closet somewhere. Either way you develop resentment and start avoiding that store or salesperson.

A different sales person sees you are looking at a product. They ask if you would like help and provide you with information about the type of item you are looking at. They then let you know that they will be just a couple of aisles over if you have more questions or need more assistance. Whether you need assistance or not, you feel empowered and cared for because you were able to make your own decisions and know that you could get help or support if you wanted it.

As you can see there is a very big difference. Being compassionate with others is not about selling them something. It is simply about making an offer to be there for them. It is about becoming aware so that you can relate to that person better and create a better experience when they are around you.

Let's say your co-worker opens up to you one day and you find out that person is going through a horrible divorce with an abusive spouse. You notice that person is extra jumpy, worn out, and their car is in the shop for repairs. You can show compassion in many ways in this situation.

You can start by making certain that you provide some space when approaching this person and approach from the front instead of from behind as much as possible. You can offer to help with some of their work if it is possible for you to do. You can offer to provide a ride to and/or from work until their car is repaired. You can make certain they have a safe place to live and offer to help them find something if needed. You can also make certain they are getting any emotional or personal support needed, such as going to a support group, and possibly offer to go with them once a week.

One of the big pieces to this is awareness. Part of awareness is understanding what someone else is going through. A victim of abuse generally will not do well around a lot of conflict or loud noises or bossy and dominating people. Many types of dyslexics don't always express things the way they mean them so it is important to clarify what they mean with what they have said, and to make certain they truly understand what you have said without being demeaning.

Sometimes you don't have the advantage of knowing what someone is going through, so learn to be aware so that you can learn how a person functions better or what works for the different people around you. With a significant other you may come to realize that they always procrastinate on certain things like dealing with customer service centers. Perhaps they have certain established routines that they will not stray from, and if they do their whole day is chaos. You learn that they need a certain amount of order, or that they need to get through their routine to have a better day.

This process of learning to be aware can take time and practice. Some things take a lot of time to notice the patterns. As mentioned in Chapter 1 it is important that when you see someone that is not going the way you think that they should that you drop the judgment and stop and start thinking that there may be a lot more going on with that person.

It is an exciting process to start waking up to being compassionate. You find that others will open up to you more. You will find that things start to flow better for you. You will notice that your relationships will get stronger and you will be able to create relationships with more people. You will start to have more inner happiness as your vibration spends more time in Love and being connected to Spirit.

Becoming aware of the numerous opportunities to be compassionate every day also raises consciousness. This opening of consciousness is likely to bring many more things your way. It is like getting a superpower of x-ray vision. You will find that you start to notice things that others don't.

Your physical body will actually start to feel lighter. Your mental body will become more attuned to the subtleties of things. Your emotional body will become more aligned with all of nature and you will be more in tune with the non-verbal signs of others. Your spiritual body will open to more experiences that create joy, laughter, love and you may even find yourself making little giggles. These giggles are the releasing of negative energy and becoming lighter.

Imagine how much more you could do if you had more information about things. Imagine how you could make wiser choices if you could see the whole picture. Now while we can't begin to truly see the whole picture; that gets very detailed and complicated. However, seeing more than what our eyes view can be a real asset.

Let's say that you needed to decide whether to let a friend stay with you for a couple of months. Your friend has only told you that things are rough at home, and she just needs somewhere that she can clear her head. As a friend you may or may not be willing to do this based on what your life is like. You may think that she can just take a vacation and doesn't really need to stay with you for a couple of months.

Now let's take that same situation and you notice that when she tells you things are rough that there is a bruise on her arm. You see that she is being very quiet and withdrawn. You then come to find out that her spouse has been physically abusing her and because she has been kept as a housewife has no way to support herself. You know that she has plenty of skills; but just needs a safe place to be while she gets out of her marriage and gets a job so that she can be on her own.

This friend deserves compassion no matter what. However, a little bit of awareness that opens up to more information for many people could make or break them offering help. To take it further, a little bit of awareness could literally save a life in a situation like this. The more compassionate we can become the more information we can receive about any given situation. The more information we have about things in our life, the smarter the choices we can make. The smarter choices we make the more fulfilling and rewarding our lives become.

How many choices would be easier for you if you had more information to work with? How would you feel if a small act by you made a huge difference in someone else's life? How would your experiences be enhanced by being more aware of the people and situations in your life?

Finding Your Truth

I remember when I got the drive to really start creating things to make a difference in people's lives, I kept being told just follow your passion. While I don't regret the many things I went through to get to where I am now; if I had really understood more about the meaning of this phrase and how to truly implement it into my life it would have been so useful. Ironically, here I am telling my clients the same thing – just follow your passion. However, one thing I have learned is that figuring out this part of the process can be very confusing and frustrating for many people.

We know that we have begun implementing compassion in our life when we get inspired to share with the world. There is a sense of knowing that you have something to give, or are here to make an impact or difference in the world. Sometimes this starts as a gentle stirring to help others. Then it grows into wanting to do it more often.

When we get this stirring of a "greater purpose" then we will notice that the mundane things aren't as fulfilling as they once were. We strive for deeper conversations and ways that we can increase our understanding of ourselves and others. As this grows more intense it may feel like it is hard to feel ok in jobs working for others or that don't provide us with creative options.

So the question becomes "so how do I find out what my passion is? How do I know what I am supposed to be doing? I feel lost and uncertain about where to go or what to do." Many of my clients have asked me these very questions. While each person needs to make this discovery on their own, I am going to try to provide some suggestions that may help you start to make your discovery and answer these questions for yourself.

So one of the first things to start with is to ask yourself what you really enjoy doing. What makes you happy to do? What would you enjoy doing even if you weren't getting paid for it? Starting here is important; because in order to make a difference in the world you need to be doing something that you really love. You must enjoy doing it even if you weren't getting paid for it.

When you understand this then the passion and enjoyment you get from doing something that you love this much, will open every opportunity to you. When you are doing what you truly love you will naturally manifest the money to go along with it. You will start to realize that you have value to give and that what you are doing is worth receiving something for it. It is OK if you decide you want to do your work for free; but the point is that you don't have to.

There are many options of what you can do from writing books, creating CD's, developing other tools or products, speaking, doing workshops, and so much more. The beauty is you get to choose what you want to do. Whether you choose to charge or not, whether you create products or not you will want to make yourself an expert on your passion. When you become an expert about your passion the more you will be able to share with others.

There is an unlimited need for people that have things to share with others. When you show up for your purpose, the universe will show up to support you in this journey. It is amazing how the universe will put people, information, and resources in your sphere to use when you make a commitment to the process. You are the creator and you get to choose how you will do it and what shape it will take.

Another thing to look at when you are trying to discover your passion and your path in this world is to ask yourself what message would you like to share with the world. If you could get people to do something, or understand something or have the opportunity to explore or do something; what would that be? Every one of us has something that we want to see in the world. It may be that you want people to have better relationships, or you want people to be able to be healthy, or maybe it is helping others do things on a low budget, or in my case it is about being compassionate.

One thing that happens when people begin on their journey is that they feel alone and lost. It is important to realize that the universe wants you to achieve your dreams, it supports you fully. How does it get any better than to know that the universe wants to help you succeed? There are also many people in this world that want you to succeed.

In order to get out of the feeling of being lost, you just need to pick one thing and start with it. It doesn't matter what that is, pick any one thing and see where it leads you. Everything is not just going to fall in your lap overnight. However, if you keep taking steps to create your desire, things will show up to help you along the way. The more steps you take the more that doors will open and people will show up to help you.

Start by asking yourself what can I do towards getting more information, or putting myself out there, or achieving my goal in the next week? What one thing can you accomplish in the next week? Is it creating a short video, or setting up a blog, or starting work on your webpage, or researching others that are doing what you are doing? Maybe it is just taking 15 minutes every morning to meditate to open your mind. It doesn't matter what it is as long as you keep taking steps.

There are numerous tools and resources out there to help you remove blocks, open doors, help you create opportunities. A simple internet search will get you started, and so many people offer free tools if you sign up for their mailing list. You don't have to make major purchases; however, if you feel that one person or another is really resonating for you then perhaps you do want to go more deeply into what they are offering. There is so much available to you if you just get started.

I have created a tool called the Genesis Clearing Statement. It helps remove blocks, provide peace within, and to create possibilities to open for you. If you would like to receive this tool you can go to my website at www.bliss.freetzi.com then you will want to email me with a request to be on my mailing list. The exciting thing about this tool is it clears the blocks that are from this lifetime, past lives, parallel lives, and even if they were genetically passed down to us. Wherever the block originated it can clear.

It is very exciting when you get started on your path. Usually once you start your journey of learning will become greatly accelerated. You will find that the universe has so much to give to you, beyond what you can imagine. The possibilities are unlimited. You get to choose how you want your experience to be.

Once you get started by discovering what really inspires you and what your message is to share with others, the next steps will keep presenting themselves for you. Getting this part of the process done is perhaps one of the most difficult parts because you have to give some very serious thought to what will work for you. This part of the process is much like writing a mission statement for a company. This can even be a great exercise to help you get focused, write a mission statement for yourself.

It is important to take steps and not try to worry about everything all at once. Doing so can overwhelm you. Keep in mind that you are going to have some challenges along the way. There are going to be days that may be frustrating; but they will pass and incredible days will come too.

Sometimes we look at the gurus that are out there and think that they have always been strong and proactive and comfortable speaking in front of large crowds. In reality many of them were terrified when they started out. Several have challenges like Dyslexia and have grown up having difficulties expressing themselves to others. All of them had fears to face along the way. All of them made mistakes along the way.

The thing that makes them different is that they chose not to buy in to the idea that they couldn't be there. They chose to believe that they could be as great as they wanted. They chose to face their fears and meet the challenges that came their way. They used these experiences to learn and grow and then turned them into tools to share with others.

This is very important to keep in mind when going through your process that not everyone is going to buy what you have to offer, not everyone is going to be as excited about what you are doing as you are, not everyone is going to agree with you. The fact is that you are not going to have 100% of the people 100% of the time; and this is OK. What these gurus do is that they focus on who they can reach. They focus on helping the people who find their information and tools useful.

It is kind of like a pulmonary specialist who doesn't try to do brain surgery; they send the patient to a brain surgeon. The pulmonary specialist focuses on those people with pulmonary issues. The message is that there is no single way that is going to work for everyone, because we are different people. So when putting a message out there, it is about putting it out there and letting whoever finds it interesting enjoy it. We have to let those that don't find it useful roll off of us, and we can offer to guide them towards something that may be more useful for them.

Remember that you have all the answers inside of you. When you search out the help of others they can help you gain perspective, put some pieces together, or trigger some inspiration; however, you are the one that really knows what will make you happy. You are the one that knows the lifestyle that you are seeking to have. You are the one that knows what will work best for you. I look forward to seeing the gift that you will share with this world. You are special, dynamic, and amazing and the world can't wait to experience what you have to offer.

Seeing With Your Heart

Have you ever wondered what it would be like if everyone cared more about a person than a policy? What if people treated you well for the sake of treating you well and not because they are getting something from you? How would it feel to be known by your name instead of a number? Who would you be if you didn't have any fears of interacting with others – would you get to know your neighbors or be friendlier with others?

These are some questions that are other ways of asking what things would be like if we learned to see with our heart. Seeing with our heart is about looking at our life, our actions, our thoughts, and our feelings from love. When we see with our heart we allow ourselves to enter a space of vulnerability and at the same time strength and confidence to place value to what is outside of ourselves. I can't help but think about how different and wonderful our world would be if we came from this space.

Many people think that if they see with their heart that they will be taken advantage of or that people won't appreciate them and what they do. These are worries that means letting everyone else have what they want while giving up everything you want. This is not the case and sometimes seeing with the heart can even require us to have "tough love" with those around us. You will still keep your boundaries, yet you may expand them to allow more to happen.

Seeing with your heart is about balancing wisdom with feeling. Enabling destructive patterns in others is not compassion or seeing with the heart. As a matter of fact seeing with the heart may require tough decisions that break the enabling pattern. Let's take a look at an example.

You find out your best friend was thrown out of where he was living and you have offered him a place to stay. After a couple of months you realize that he has not gone on a single job interview, has not done anything except sit around watching t.v. He has not offered to pay you anything because he has no money. You offer to help him get his act together and spend time helping him prepare for interviews, and give him money to eat on and get some new clothes to give a better presentation. Still he does nothing.

Continuing to give him a place to live and food to eat is enabling the pattern of doing nothing. Now many would really struggle with saying you can't bear to see this friend homeless and starving; however, they are completely living off of you. At this point compassion would lend to giving him room and board only in exchange for doing something – even if that is cleaning the house, keeping up the yard work, or doing other things that will be useful to you. On the other hand if this friend refuses this and you cannot afford to support him, allowing him to remain at your home is only enabling him in the destructive pattern.

This is where the "tough love" factor comes in. As long as someone is willing to pay for everything and allow him to do nothing he will continue on this destructive path. While it is hard to put your friend out, he needs to learn how to take care of himself. You can offer to be there for emotional support. If this friend still does nothing after leaving your home it is important to keep in mind that this is his choice. He has the choice to make changes, he doesn't have to live a rough life.

When we look at this on a more universal scale that it takes five positives to counteract a negative and 20 positives to create progression from a negative; it then shows that it takes five to twenty people to offset the choices of this one friend. Only by your friend choosing to change and step into being creative instead of destructive can we progress as a whole universe. So enabling your friend not only is destructive on him but puts you feeding what is destructive and will drain you as well. This means that by enabling him twelve to forty two people are affected.

Now expanding on this situation you could also offer a different option to your friend, knowing that he has so much negativity in his life and needs things to be shifted so that he is completely surrounded by positive energy. This could include finding a church or other charity organization that is focused on helping others, or that doesn't allow negativity in it's culture. This can be another opportunity to work for room and board. For some this may work and for others it may not; however, it is a possible option to putting your friend out to completely be on their own. This works in that many of these situations have people that can provide more full time interaction, and where some of the distractions such as t.v. are removed.

Now that we have discussed a situation about keeping boundaries and getting past the blur of helping and enabling others; let's look at what it would be like if more people could see with their heart. For many people this may seem like only a dream world; however, with every person that chooses to operate this way the easier it gets for everyone and the more enjoyable life becomes for everyone. When we see with the heart our heart opens, and as discussed earlier in this book it only takes one person to start being this way to have it cascade into a global impact. When we talk of one person making a global impact it means that they serve as a trigger for bigger events it does not mean that they do everything on their own.

Let's take a look at what the world would be like if everyone learned to see with their heart. Animal cruelty would be non-existent. Older people in nursing homes would never be lonely. Bullies wouldn't run our lives. Everyone would have enough to have a comfortable lifestyle. Our neighborhoods would be safe. We would have balance in our lives, providing enough time for work, sleep, family, relationships, and ourselves. People would be courteous and helpful. "Big brother" wouldn't need to watch us because we would be watching over ourselves. Homelessness, hunger and crime would become as rare as the rarest diseases.

This is only a few of the things; but the list is limitless. Imagine what your life could be like simply by seeing from the heart and having others see you from their heart? Imagine the lives that you could change by doing this one simple thing. So how can we get to seeing with our heart? It is about being willing to let go of things that seem important but really aren't in a situation. It is about shifting how we view things in order to create a positive influence or outcome in the things that happen in our lives and with the people that are in our lives, even with those that we don't know.

When you learn to see with your heart you stop worrying about how true a statement is and start looking at what is needed in the situation. Let's say you have an employee that needs some time off. This employee tells you they have a doctor's appointment, when in reality they just needed a couple of extra hours that day to handle something in their life. Now most employers get hung up on whether the employee actually had a doctor's appointment. Someone seeing from the heart isn't concerned with that; but shifts their view to ask the employee if everything is alright with them and are they going to be able to work now that they are there.

The key is, it is not important whether the employee actually went to see a doctor. What is important is that the employee feels that they were able to do what they needed to put themselves into a space that allowed them to be better at work. What is more valuable to the work environment an employee that is distracted and worried about something outside of work or an employee that is at peace and ready to work? Now if this became a pattern of the employee always running late, then the needs of the employee and the company need to be addressed.

What concerns me is that when people feel like they have to lie in order to "justify" their actions to someone or to cover doing something to take care of themselves, this is feeding destructive and not creative energy. It also shows that we are not caring about the needs of people enough. There are always workable options and solutions but many companies have gotten stuck in rigid ways that make it difficult and challenging to get things done. Companies have gotten away from respecting and valuing their employees and feeling like they are doing them a favor to give them a job.

In days gone by employers and employees had a mutual respect for each other and many things were able to be created. Employees felt like they had a voice, they were shown and given appreciation daily, there were bonuses and gifts to show they were valued. Employers were given loyalty, devotion, honesty, and efforts were made by employees to do a good job and accomplish as much as possible. Today it has become a very self-focused gimme environment for most places. The employers are one step away from being a sweat shop even if everyone wears suits; and employees are doing as little as possible to keep their job. Today's strategy is a destructive environment which is causing bankruptcy, layoffs, buyouts and closures.

It really comes down to an old adage of being the change that you want to see. If you knew your neighbor was sick during a snow storm and you had the time to plow their driveway and sidewalks, would you do it? Would you want someone to do this for you? If your spouse was having a long tough day would you be willing to cook dinner or take them out or give them a massage? How would it feel if someone did that for you? If your friend showed up at your house in tears needing to talk would you make the time? Would you want them to help you in need?

If we want a world that is different from what we have, then it is up to us to do the things that will change it into the world we want. We cannot worry about how many people are ready to join us, we just have to know that it starts with us. When others see us being different, then one or two will also want to be different. As those one or two become different, more will want to join in. So this progresses to where almost everyone is choosing this different way of being. All we have to do is choose the difference and everything else happens.

Seeing with our heart means we choose to be the life we want to live. It means that we look at what needs to happen instead of getting stuck in unimportant details. It is about being willing and available to make a difference in the lives of others. We are living to strengthen the creative and loving energy of the whole. We are considering others and not just ourselves.

What is the life that you want to live? How will you make a difference? Whose life will you have a positive affect on? Why would you surround yourself with negative people that drag you down when you can surround yourself with positive people that help you succeed? When will you get started on living the life you really want to live?

Loving Self

Have you ever noticed that it is really hard to cheer someone else up when your life feels like it is falling apart? How much do you feel you can give to others when you are tired, drained, and worrying about how you are going to make it to tomorrow? Of course it is going to be difficult to have an open mind and be there for others when you have not gotten things together in your own life.

When you feel sick the last thing you want to do is be around others. When we are not taking the time to love ourselves it is much like being sick. You don't want to be around others and they don't want to be around you.

One of the things I have heard from people is that they feel guilty when they do things for themselves. Many have a perception that doing things for your own enjoyment and pleasure is selfish. Some have even gone as far as to say to love one's self is to feed the ego and is a sin. On the other hand I could argue that many things we do for others and neglecting our own needs and care is selfish.

These terms can be confusing because it is all about how they are used and perceived. Selfishness can mean acting without any consideration of others. It can be the person that lets a door slam in someone's face instead of holding it open until they get through. It can mean taking the last item on the shelf by cutting in front of someone and pushing them aside just to get it. However, it can also mean taking time for the self in order to restore or improve circumstances or bring peace and calmness. This can be the person that takes a few minutes every morning to meditate so that they will have a calm, alert, and peaceful mind.

I am not interested in hashing out terms and all of their variances. The key is that loving yourself is a necessary and valuable piece to activating compassion and living a life that you love. What if taking fifteen minutes for yourself every morning and every evening allowed everything in your day to flow smoothly, allowed you to have more confidence in yourself, brought achievements every day, allowed you to sleep better, allowed everything that you want and need to flow into your life quickly and easily? Well this is exactly what happens when you take time to love yourself.

So you may be wondering how to go about creating greater love for yourself. What I love about this is that it can be done as part of your everyday life or in combination with other things that you may already do. It doesn't have to take a huge amount of time or energy. Let's look at some of the ways that we can show love to ourselves.

How we eat is one key way to loving yourself. Think about it. If you had a child that was allergic to certain foods would you still feed them those foods? Would you let your children eat only candy and fast food? Of course not because you love them too much to let them destroy their health that way. It takes the same amount of energy to pick up foods that will help you as it does to pick up foods that are detrimental to your health. Often times I find that eating healthy is actually easier to prepare than most unhealthy foods.

What you do when you aren't working is another way of loving yourself. Would you want or allow your kids to sit inside doing nothing but watching t.v. when they weren't in school? Of course you wouldn't and there is no need to do it to yourself. It is important to have variety in our routine and to move and do things. Now of course we all need some time to just relax; but the key is to balance our t.v. time with other things. For example after dinner, clean up the dishes and then go for a walk before settling in front of the t.v. Go to the gym before or after work. Step outside and breathe some fresh air before going to bed. These are only a few examples to get your mind thinking.

Now work, something that consumes at least one third of the day at least five days a week. For many people it is consuming as much as two thirds of the day seven days a week. These days people feel very pressured to work more and more just to make ends meet. It is important that as a part of loving yourself you start to make the shift to ask yourself how to work smarter instead of harder. There are several studies out there that show that when we work excessively we are cutting into our sleep and our bodies then breakdown from not having enough opportunities to restore itself. Start looking for ways to get yourself back to a forty hour or less work week with at least two days off in a row. Even if you don't get there overnight, keep taking the steps to get yourself there. This may mean living more frugally or paying off debts or taking in a roommate. There are many options if you just put your mind to it.

Dress for success. As part of loving yourself look at the way you dress. Are you happy with the clothes you put on? Do they give you a feeling of being put together? Do they express your personality? When we like what we are wearing and it is appropriate to what we are doing we will improve our interactions with others and increase our confidence which leads to being more successful in our day. When you wear things that make you look "dumpy" or "sloppy" or are like wearing pajamas it actually will drain your energy and breakdown your self-esteem. If you don't have a talent for picking out things that look good, find someone around you that does and ask them to go shopping for new clothes with you. The more you feel comfortable in what you are wearing the better you will present yourself.

Give yourself a beauty day. Men need to do this too. It is important to take the time to file your nails, do a facial, moisturize your skin. Many of these things you can even do while watching your favorite t.v. show. When you do things to improve your "beauty" or to pamper yourself, you will also develop feelings of being youthful which also leads you to feel more energetic. Imagine if you could completely restore your energy by soaking your feet in oil or wearing a facial mask for fifteen minutes.

Clear your mind. This technique is simply about taking time to clear out the worries, concerns, or any unsettling events of the day. It can also be a way to prep yourself for anything that you need to take care of during the day. Some people prefer to do this as meditation or yoga or simply by breathing. The key is that you give yourself a quiet place where you can consciously see yourself succeeding in your day or letting go of things that have happened during the day. It is also good to use some time at the end of the day to acknowledge 10 things that were great about your day or that you have to be grateful for.

Along with clearing your mind is to shift from negative to positive thoughts. The more our mind is focused on positive things the more support we develop and the more we can create experiences that we love. This is probably one of the easiest things to incorporate. For example while brushing your teeth you can be saying to yourself "I love my outfit" or "I am full of energy today" or any other statement you like. You can also say things like "I am a successful employee" or "my boss loves the work I do" while on your way to work. Running messages like this all throughout your day will keep you providing constant love to yourself.

Imagine if you felt loved in everything that you did? Imagine if you felt constantly surrounded in loving energy? Imagine if every time you did something to love yourself something good happened? Imagine that the more you love yourself the more others love you too?

Remember giving starts at home, and home is within your own self. We need to be willing to not make excuses for ourselves but to be forgiving of any shortcomings, misunderstandings, or mishaps that occur. We are not perfect, but we can be perfectly ourselves.

How many times have you been harsh with yourself, calling yourself stupid or feeling you are inadequate because you made a mistake or didn't catch something or didn't succeed at something? How many times have you let yourself feel like a failure because things didn't work out a particular way? How many times have you told a friend different when they felt like this? Part of becoming a compassionate person is being compassionate with your own self.

We can let go of these personal judgments by acknowledging that we are going to make mistakes from time to time and it is going to be ok. To say next time I will be better. To learn from what didn't work instead of getting angry about it. It is about forgiving yourself. Wouldn't you forgive a friend if they made a mistake? Of course you would, and likewise you need to forgive yourself.

I often times like to take that situation that I made a mistake with and make light of it. I like to find ways to laugh at myself instead of getting upset about things. The fact is that it happened and now it is over and done with; it is in the past. I may not be able to undo it; but I can choose to move forward and not let it hold me down.

For example, I might have told a friend that I was going to meet them at 11:00am. I head off to take care of things before I go and lose track of time. When I realize that I messed up by doing other things, I choose to call that friend and let them know that I messed up in gauging my time and am running late and acknowledge that their time is valuable. In the course of this call I may choose to lighten the situation and my mistake by saying something like "there I was trying to be efficient and just got totally lost – I am really going to have to work on this time efficiency thing. Next time I will leave a couple of hours early and hang out."

With this I have not demeaned myself, simply stuck to the facts of the situation, taken accountability for my actions, recognized the other person's time as valuable, and eased the tension off of the situation. I am not making excuses for my actions, but owning them. Usually when I have done this it becomes a source of joking and fun in later interactions. Being able to laugh at ourselves can change any tense frustrating situation into something that is easy to deal with and restores comfort.

What ways will you choose to show you that you love you? How can you be more forgiving of your own self and the things that you do? Will you start loving you as much as you possibly can?

Loving Others

In addition to loving ourselves it is important to learn about loving others. This is not just about significant others or spouses or even family; but encompasses everyone that we know. Now just because we learn to love others doesn't mean that you have to become best friends with everyone that you meet. There are always going to be people we get along with and those that challenge us. The key comes in learning to love others even if they are not someone that we choose to hang out with.

I know that it is truly possible to love everyone. I can already hear the comments saying "can you love the serial killer? How about the wife beater? And the drug dealers?" and most likely there are many more. Actually yes, I can love each and every one of these people. The reason that I can do this is because I have learned to separate the person from the actions. I may completely disagree with their actions; but the people themselves I sincerely love.

Now some are saying but the person is the choices that they make and the decisions that they make. While I understand this thinking pattern, if I followed it then I could argue that no one deserves to be loved as we have all made poor choices and bad decisions at one point or another in our lives. I can count several that I have made. When I look at the core of what is going on with these people they have value and skills just like everyone else, they need to be loved like everyone else, and like everyone else once they have fully lived in love and have been loved truly and fully they would not make those decisions.

The people that are facing these kinds of struggles are much like a child that needs extra help learning. Now I do not believe that their actions are justified or excusable by any means. However, I do believe that they need extra help learning how to be loving, or to gain control over their habits or emotions. When I see these people what I am really seeing is the essence of what is around them which includes things like pain, fear, abandonment, frustration, and more.

Now yes, I do admit that sometimes people have chemical or physical issues going on that need to be dealt with; but I also feel that with providing them with what they need on all levels there would be wiser choices being made. Now these are extreme levels of people but the basis is the same with people that struggle financially, or are trying to do things that they haven't learned. Do we get appalled with a child for falling off their bike? Do we blame someone for not working when no one has taught them how to interview or fill out an application?

I think of the movie Trading Places with Dan Aykroyd and Eddie Murphy. This movie shows that simply by having people that show you everything and work with you that someone's life can be completely changed. It also shows how that even someone with plenty of skills and knowledge when left on their own and ignored can make one bad choice after another.

Now we can all sit around making excuses for why we do what we do and why we are what we are; however, the reality is that we can change this at any time. People are doing it every single day, making the choice to be different. However, we also make the choice to not change or be a victim to our circumstances and to wallow in excuses.

Now when we look at loving others the key concept that I have learned is to accept them for who they are and then love them anyway. This is where unconditional loving or compassionate loving comes in. This concept has probably been most associated in love relationships. The key for me is to let this be in all areas of life and with everyone around us.

To get to this stage of acceptance is to learn to celebrate our differences, be compassionate to circumstances, support others in making improvements and personal development, acknowledge their assets and gifts that they have to share with the world, learn how you can bring out their gifts, and let others be who they are. We all have things that make us unique and special. Having differences allows us to learn and expand beyond ourselves. Almost everyone has had some tough times in their life and struggled, having someone who is understanding and caring in these times and that knows we will come out of the challenges provides strength to stand up and face the world again. It changes lives.

It is important that even when you have not gotten along with someone in the past, that you support them when they are ready to make changes and improve themselves personally. As a compassionate being we are willing to put the past behind us and support what we know will be best for the whole. Wouldn't you want someone to help you if you were making changes?

This is like being in high school and never being accepted. Then when you go back to a reunion you find out the person that bullied you is trying to build an animal rescue center and develop community events to save animals from abuse. You have a choice to hold a grudge and simply say "well good luck with that" while whispering under your breath "I hope he fails miserably" or you can put the past behind you and say "I think that is amazing work, and so glad that you are working to help the animals that cannot help themselves. I am really happy to see the changes you have made and hope that you are very successful in your endeavors." It is important for ourselves and the whole that we support these changes and encourage others to stay on a path that will help us all, no matter how they used to be. Remember once it is in the past it no longer truly exists, for only this moment exists.

Every person has gifts and assets, even if they don't use them to benefit others. When loving others the key with this aspect is to be aware of what gifts and assets others have. What sometimes rubs us the wrong way can still be a very useful gift and provide tons of information of what is going on with someone, which in turns helps us to understand them, their needs, and how to interact with them better.

For example a bully has skills of organizing people, taking charge, and making decisions. These are great skills and the key is to understand the fears and pain behind the bully. Once done, then change can occur and their skills can be used for something really valuable. We find a way to express our skills and if we are not using these skills for something helpful then they will manifest in destructive ways, especially if other negative emotions such as pain and fear are present.

In my years of working with people I have found that one thing that is at our core is that we want to be able to be ourselves. We don't want others telling us how to be or who to be or what to be. There is a need to make these choices on our own. In loving others we can offer a different way of being to someone that appears to be taking a downward spiral or that is wrapped up in frustration or other negative emotions.

Sometimes it seems to me that we are more accepting of friends being who they are than we are of significant others or spouses or family. I can't count the number of times that I have seen people trying to change the person that they claim to love. If we really want people to change, it is important to first accept them for who they are and not expect them to change. By expecting someone to change or demanding them to change they are likely to rebel and not want to consider other options.

How would you feel if someone said I love you, but you need to change your religion and your hairstyle and the clothes you wear and how you interact with people and how you hold your silverware when you eat? If you are like many people you would not be feeling very loved. Change is not something to be forced, but is something to be embraced. Many people are very open to being different and making changes as long as they don't feel that it is a requirement to be with someone.

When we love others as a compassionate being, we can look at all the little things that are a part of who they are and say "yes, he does procrastinate" or "she always spends an hour getting ready" or one of many other little traits; but I love that person with all their little quirks and characteristics. When you can say, "I welcome and support any changes they choose to make; but love them just the way they are" and really feel and mean it, then you are loving others from compassion.

Every person is filled with beauty, gifts, skills, challenges, circumstances, lessons. None of us are perfect; but we are all perfectly imperfect. Can you find and see these things in the people you know? Can you help them be aware of these things in themselves without judging or being critical? Will you recognize the beauty and gifts and skills that each person around you has?

Take some time to reflect and see where you need to be more accepting with the people that you know. Can you imagine how great it would be if everyone around you could accept you for who you are and provide options for you to do and learn things the way that works best for you? How amazing would it be if everyone around you supported you in your growth and acknowledged and utilized your skills and gifts? How much more empowered would you feel from having this? Start giving this to others and you will find they will also give it back to you.

Making A Difference

This chapter is for those that are feeling really ready to become proactive with creating compassion in their own life and in helping others. Most religions and spiritual philosophies talk about moving into a life of service and out of selfishness. For many people this can be a very scary thought, I know it has been for me. The reason for this is that many people have associated service with rigid definitions of preaching, or being a wandering prophet, or other such traditional paths.

I know for me when I first thought about the concept of service these were the pictures that first came into my mind. As devoted as I am, honestly I just couldn't see myself in those formal capacities. I then started to reflect back on the teachings of Isaiah in which service was about being a messenger, a living example. Isaiah chose to reach out to people in ways that worked for them and not just by traditional means.

When I think of this concept I feel that this is where more and more people relate. It is a way of serving outside of some of the traditional religious viewpoints. Actually, most of us exist in service; we just haven't recognized it as being that.

Let's look at the mother and homemaker. For years there was no real credit given to this role; although there are a couple of belief systems that find this to be a very "holy" role. The person choosing to take this path is completely of service to her family, wiping the tears, motivating during the tough times, devoting time for school projects, guiding while her children grow up, and so much more. If it weren't for those serving in this way, it would be much more difficult to get help on committees and organizations, and think of how often they were the ones willing to watch over other people's children or be the one hosting the sleepovers allowing other parents to have a break for a night.

How about all of the people in so called "unglorious" positions such as janitors, maids, groundskeepers, dishwashers, and so on? All of these people provide service by accepting a job that most people do not want to do. Some of these people got in them by circumstances, some because they were willing to take anything in order to support a spouse or aging parents, some simply to have something to do. No matter what the reason, these people have as much to teach us as anyone. My experience is that they keep their life simple, most of them have a much stronger balance in their life than most corporate executives. The point is they too are of service in keeping things in a state for others to enjoy them.

No matter what the profession or life that someone has chosen they are in service whether they have recognized it or not. Just think of how much teachers serve us, or businesses, massage therapists, inventors. Really every one of us is already acting in service to others whether it is obvious or not. Every one of us is contributing and doing something that helps others.

Ok, there are probably a couple of you thinking "what about my boyfriend, he won't do anything, he doesn't work all he does is sit around all day. What service could he possibly be providing?" So this service is one type of service that is usually never recognized as a service. The service of those that seem to be doing nothing is to teach us to find ways to motivate and assist them to find purpose and meaning in life. So in essence their service is in bringing out service in others. Now I am not saying that you should surround yourself by people doing nothing with their life, as that could be a whole other book; but there is still value, purpose, and service even in these people that can be frustrating for us to deal with.

Now that you are realizing that consciously or unconsciously we are all in service in one way or another, we can progress on. So the key now is that we want to raise our consciousness of how to be of service beyond our everyday responsibilities or roles. So while you may provide service during the course of your work day, how do you provide service when you are not at work?

To be proactive in being of service to others means that you are ready to help others in any way that you can whenever you can. Now I am not saying you have to put your life completely on hold for everyone else (although if you choose to do this that is up to you – however, that is beyond what most people are ready for or what most people are able to do). What you are doing at this stage is learning to take advantage of opportunities that come to you to help. The key here is that you are willing to take advantage of opportunities to be of service.

Now just because you offer, doesn't mean that everyone is going to take you up on that offer. This is ok if they don't take you up, there is no reason to feel offended or upset; because the important part is that you made the offer. Many people will say that they are ready to move forward or do something in their life; but when given the assistance or opportunity to do it, they disappear or pull away and don't take advantage of it.

Not too long ago I had someone telling me they were ready to get a better job; but couldn't find anything. They had a list of reasons why they couldn't, but had one in particular that they felt was holding them back. I offered to co-create something with them so that they could get the experience needed. I never heard back from this person. What this shows is that this person was not ready for the successes that they thought they were, at least not at this time. Some people are simply afraid of succeeding (again this could be a whole other book), so when they are given the opportunity to make things happen they pull away. Again do not take offense to this, when they are ready they will either make things happen or find someone that will help them.

Now the key is for you to raise your consciousness to be aware of opportunities for being of service. This comes from simply listening, watching and paying attention to what others are sharing with you. You might hear someone say "I really want to learn how to do _____" or "I wish I knew how to make _____ happen" or "my dream is to _____" and other similar statements.

Sometimes what the person is trying to accomplish is something that you have no knowledge about. You can still offer to help them find some connections if you are feeling driven or refer them to someone that may be able to help them. Even a referral can turn out to be a great service to someone. On the other hand many times you very well may have experience or knowledge that can be useful to the person, and help them accomplish what they are trying to do. You can offer to sit down and share what you do know or to show them how to go about succeeding.

Now one thing to be careful of when trying to be of service with someone is to not force your ideas onto them. Offer your assistance and ask if they would like you to help. Another thing to be careful of is to not do things for them. Remember they want it to be their accomplishment not yours.

Now you can lend a helping hand or help them pull together supplies and resources to make the accomplishment or work with them, but do not completely do it for them. The key is to help them learn, grow, and develop themselves. Now there is an exception to this. The exception is when the service is all about doing something for someone. This would include picking up some groceries for someone that is home sick, or mowing the lawn for an elderly neighbor, or giving a co-worker a ride to work when their car is broken down.

Every day we are presented with opportunities to be of service to others if we open ourselves to being aware of them. What is exciting to me is when I am able to take advantage of these opportunities to serve. It brings a sense of renewal, joy, and fulfillment. What is exciting is that often times there are also many residual benefits that you will receive from being of service to others.

When we are able to be of service to others we are raising our vibration to a space of love or above. When we do this, we naturally become a magnet for many wonderful things to come into our lives. You are likely to notice that things start working in your favor, or others are willing to help you, or you may draw people into your life that are useful to you. You also will find that all areas of your life will improve from being in this space which includes love, relationships, finances, career.

Think about all the opportunities that come your way every day to be of service. If you miss an opportunity you may be able to make an offer when you do become aware of it; or simply be aware of it and use it to learn how to increase your awareness. How great will you feel knowing that you have made a difference in someone's life and helped them to achieve a dream? Again you don't want to overwhelm yourself in the process of being of service. It can sometimes be good to set small goals and develop from there when becoming proactive in being of service. For example, try offering to be of service once a week and then after awhile you can develop it to being more frequent.

Creating A New World

In the last chapter I discussed ways to become more proactive in being of service. Now we are ready to look at what it is like to really live from compassion. I don't expect everyone to get here overnight, for I feel taking a path of living compassion is an ongoing process. There are many who feel as if they can't be in compassion all the time. This is why I suggest developing it in small steps that are comfortable for you.

Starting this process is much like a baby that sees others walking, but has barely learned to sit on their own. The baby has to start by lying and observing what is around it. It then gets to a point where it learns to lift itself a little. Soon it can sit on it's own. This is followed by learning to crawl, stand and then walk. When the baby is still thinking about walking it can't imagine that it will be able to stand for long periods of time or even run. However, with each step that it takes it gets closer.

As we learn to move into a compassionate life we find that life continues to grow even better. We create a spiral of positive emotions and experiences within ourselves and others. We set forth a chain of events that benefits numerous people and not just the people and situations that we are in service with. Our life really begins to change into a space of great fulfillment and enlightenment.

Many people have asked me what their path is. Learning to live a compassionate life is one of the best ways that I know of to find your path and what you should be doing in the world. Finding one's path is about taking what you love to do more than anything or using the message that you most want to world to experience and learning to put it in a form that is useful, helpful and of service to others. It is looking at what you most want to share with this world.

The more we refine our skills of being compassionate, the more we learn what we want to do and what will fulfill us. The more that each one of us steps onto our path and starts to share our gifts with others, the more we step into living a compassionate life. This is an amazing and blessed cycle to experience. The feelings of happiness and fulfillment, achievement and love that go with living a compassionate life is something that I want everyone to be able to experience.

The more people that choose to live compassion, the more the world can change into an enjoyable experience. When we change ourselves into compassionate beings we change the world. You will be creating a new and wonderful world in your own life and in the bigger whole. I would like to share with you a story from a friend of mine which I find to be a wonderful sample of someone who is living from compassion.

"Here's a story I know you would appreciate. Our next door neighbor growing up in Manhattan Beach, was like a second mom to us kids. She and her husband were just great people and put up with all of us kids and our crazy stuff. Then we all grew up and didn't keep in touch with her. I later found out her husband died. My parents also sold their house and moved and didn't keep in touch with her. Then one day about 4 years ago, I sent her a letter. She called me in tears because she was so glad to hear from me. I went to her house and we reconnected. I set up a reunion party with her and my family. It was a beautiful thing. My dad cried at the party as well as a lot of us. She was 93 years old and could barely see but she still had that spunky character. Well, 4 months later my oldest sister died, then she died, then my dad died. I later thought that was a beautiful thing we all experienced.

These are the kinds of things people like you and I do and appreciate the value. I try to do things for others that gives them something no one else usually does. A small moment or moments of making them feel loved, laugh, appreciate life in a way they maybe never have or seldom do. "

I really appreciate my friend taking the time to share this story with me and for giving me approval to share it with you. It really shows the mindset of a compassionate person. Any opportunity to create a small moment that leads to someone feeling loved, laughing, or helps them to appreciate and experience life in a different way is such a blessing for everyone involved. I think what if my friend hadn't taken this initiative? What if he had waited to take action? The compassionate person learns to follow the inner voice that guides and leads them to take these actions.

What contribution will you make? Are you ready to find your life purpose? What if everyone was living compassion? How will you start living compassion now?

Appendix

Summary Steps For Activating Compassion

1) Get rid of judgments
2) Care about others while they are going through their challenges
3) Tell others what you need and want from them. Give to yourself.
4) It doesn't have to hurt
5) True and compassionate giving allows you to receive more than you can give.
6) Be willing to see, hear, and open enough to learn from all situations
7) Build your awareness to awaken your compassion
8) Know what you want to share with the world and what your message is
9) Be the change you want to see
10) Take time to love you all throughout your day in multiple ways
11) Accept others for who they are and love them anyway
12) Learn to be aware and take advantage of opportunities to be of service
13) What new world will you create for yourself and those around you?

About the Author

I am Jesse Ann Nichols George, an Integrated Development Specialist. My work encompasses multiple fields of study and belief systems to help people create the life they desire to live. The work I do comes from:

- a lifetime of study through personal experiences

- channeling past lives and, ancestor support – I am a 13+ generation spiritual advisor, energy tuner, life/relationship/spiritual and wellness coach, wholistic and natural lifestyle advisor

- working with clients to achieve desired results and work through life processes for over 30 years

- researching and studying the influences of environment, communications, personal dynamics, past lives, religions, cultural beliefs and lifestyles, metaphysics, wholistic healing, energetics, quantum energy, herbs, astrology, numerology, fengshui, environmental design, signs and symbols, dreams and dream work, meditation and visualization, mantras/chanting/affirmations, paranormal activity and spirit communication, auras, tantra, relationships, chakras, intuition and psychic work, crystals and gemstones, tarot, past life regression, divining, laying on of hands and energy alignment

- 13 years of producing my own astrological forecast, hand casting charts, and during part of this time also had my own weekly radio segment for astrology

- Being a guest on radio stations

- Being interviewed on tv on wiccan practices

- Working on missing person cases

- Teaching courses on multiple subjects

- Creating spiritual tools and products

- Owning and operating a retail store for herbs and other spiritual products

I continue to develop, enhance, and embrace my gifts during this journey on earth and beyond.

"Open your heart to love, embrace it, become it: and you will find all things are possible."

Jesse has studied from a variety of teachers – many of them being Masters; some have chosen to remain very hidden and personally hand select their students, some carry more notoriety, some came from a lineage who did their work, channeling other planes and lifetimes. Jesse looks to all her teachers – past, present, and future - with gratitude for time, experiences, wisdom, and willingness to share, believe, and support her.

Jesse's work has led her to work with people from a variety of cultures, backgrounds, and ages. She has worked with abuse victims, parents with troubled teens, counselors and therapists, professors and teachers, politicians, spiritual leaders, other healers, heads of companies, actors/actresses/those in the entertainment industry, writers, lawyers, artists and more.

"Appreciate all that life has to offer you at any moment, and you will not be disappointed."

Connect With Jesse

If you would like to connect with me there are many ways that you can do this:

Sign up for my mailing list by sending an email with your name and the email that you want the mailings sent to. Send your request to lifeofbliss@q.com

Follow my blog at www.getyourblisson.tumblr.com

Connect with me on LinkedIn at
www.linkedin.com/in/spiritualadvisorjesse

Connect with me on Twitter at
www.twitter.com/#!/JesseNicholsGeo

Connect with me on Facebook at
www.facebook.com/profile.php?id=100003558041413

Made in the USA
Charleston, SC
06 May 2012